The Buddha
History's First Humanist

THE BUDDHA

HISTORY'S FIRST HUMANIST

•

Life-Story

For the new generation every where

A Ist Century Classic
by the celebrated Sanskrit

ASHVA GHOSA

Translated into easy to understand English
by the Oxford Scholar

E.H. JOHNSTON

from Indian, Tibetan and Chinese Sources

Reader-friendly
Millennium Three Editions

VIJAY GOEL
English-Hindi Publisher

S-16, Naveen Shahdara, Delhi-110032, India
E mail: goelbooks@rediffmail.com

ISBN: 81-89297-36-8

Edition: 2018

The present
Millennium Three / 21st Century Edition

Published by
VIJAY GOEL
English-Hindi Publisher

S-16, Navin Shahdara
Delhi-110032, India
Phone: 22324833; 9810461412
email: goelbooks@rediffmail.com

Typeset at :
Computek System
Naveen Shahdara, Delhi-110032

Printed at :
Sharma Printers, Delhi

PREFACE

The formation and growth of any religion is bound to have a cultural background. This is revealed by the widespread interest in Lord Buddha and his philosophy with the result that Buddhism has now spread all over the world. Its inception in India was followed by its transmission to China and now in the 20th century, it has attracted followers all over the world, especially in the countries of Asia, Europe and America. Lumbini, Bodh Gaya, Kapilavastu, Rajgir and Sarnath are the most important places in India and Nepal, associated with Lord Buddha.

But for a solid understanding of Buddhism in its various contemporary forms, it is very necessary to know and understand the basis and origins of the stories about the life of Shakamuni Gautama Buddha, the founder of Buddhism. Alongside, we have also to understand the cultural and religious setting in India because of which the initial rise of Buddhism took place in the country.

As a matter of fact, we must appreciate and understand the close connection between the personal history of the founder and the religion which he established. While everyone knows the high standing of the family - the nobility - to which Gautam Buddha was born, on the other hand, the most important factor is how Shakamuni spurned all that glamour of being a crown prince and chose the path of the monastic system. So before studying a religion, we must understand the life of its founder.

Through the present book, the authors have tried to acquaint the readers with the life story of Gautama Buddha, the first humanist of history. This life story of the first

Humanist in world history has been covered in 28 chapters.

The birth and life in a palace is followed by flight in search of God. Then comes the story of his resistance to pleas for returning to the life in the palace. This is followed by his enlightenment and conversion leading to the great disciples, who followed his principles and message towards *Nirvana*. This is followed by a story of the Relics and Eulogy and finally ends with the rise of Ashoka, who was devoted to the faith.

We are sure, readers all around shall use this book for understanding contemporary Buddhism in its varied forms.

—Editors

CONTENTS

1

BIRTH

There was a king of the unconquerable Sakyas, Suddhodana by name, of the race of Iksvaku and the peer of Iksvaku in might. Pure he was in conduct and beloved of his people as the moon in autumn.

That counterpart of Indra had a queen, a very Saci, whose splendour corresponded to his might. In beatury like Padma, in steadfastness like the earth, she was called Mahamaya, from her resemblance to the incomparable Maya.

This ruler of men, dallying with his queen, enjoyed, as it were, the sovereign glory of Vaisravana. Then without defilement she received the fruit of the womb, just as knowledge united with mental concentration bears fruit.

Before she conceived, she saw in her sleep a white lord of elephants entering her body, yet she felt thereby no pain.

Maya, the queen of that god-like king, bore in her womb the glory of her race and, being in her purity free from weariness, sorrow and illusion, she set her mind on the sin-free forest.

In her longing for the lonely forest as suited to trance, she asked the king to go and stay in the grove called Lumbini, which was gay like the garden of Caitraratha, with trees of every kind.

The lord of the earth, full of wonder and joy, recognized that her disposition was noble from her possession of piety, and left the fortunate city, in order to gratify her, not for a pleasure excursion.

In that glorious grove the queen perceived that the time

of her delivery was at hand and, amidst the welcome of thousands of waiting-women, proceeded to a couch overspread with an awning.

Then as soon as Pusya became propitious, from the side of the queen, who was hallowed by her vows, a son was born for the weal of the world, without her suffering either pain or illness.

As was the birth of Aurva from the thigh, of Prthu from the hand, of Mandhatr, the peer of Indra, from the head, of Kaksivat from the armpit, on such vise was his birth.

When in due course he had issued from the womb, he appeared as if he had descended from the sky, for he did not come into the world through the portal of life; and, since he had purified his being through many aeons, he was born not ignorant but fully conscious.

With his lustre and steadfastness he appeared like the young sun come down to earth, and despite this his dazzling brilliance, when gazed at, held all eyes like the moon.

For with the glowing radiance of his limbs he eclipsed, like the sun, the radiance of the lamps, and, beauteous with the hue of precious gold, he illumined all the quarters of space.

He who was like the constellation of the Seven Seers walked seven steps with such firmness that the feet were lifted up unwavering and straight and that the strides were long and set down firmly.

And looking to the four quarters with the bearing of a lion, he uttered a speech proclaiming the truth : "I am born for Enlightenment for the good of the world; this is my last birth in the world of phenomena."

Two streams of water, clear as the rays of the moon and having the virtue, one of heat, one of cold, poured forth from the sky and fell on his gracious head to give his body refreshment by their contact.

He lay on a couch with a gorgeous canopy, feet of beryl and framework glistening with gold, and round him the Yaksa lords stood reverently on guard with golden lotuses in their hands.

The dwellers in heaven, themselves remaining invisible, held up in the sky a white umbrella and, bowing their heads in obeisance before his majesty, muttered the highest blessings that he might obtain Enlightenment.

The mighty snakes in their thirst for the most excellent Law fanned him and, with eyes shining with devotion, bestrewed him with *manddra* flowers, offices they had performed for the Buddhaa of the past.

And gladdened by the virtue of his birth in this fashion, the Suddhadhivasa deities rejoiced in their pure natures, though passion was extinct in them, for the sake of the world drowned in suffering.

At his birth the earth, nailed down as it was with the king of mountains, trembled like a ship struck by the wind; and from the cloudless sky there fell a shower perfumed with sandalwood and bringing blue and pink lotuses.

Delightful breezes blew, soft to the touch and wafting down heavenly raiment; the very sun shone more brightly and the fire, unstirred, blazed with gracious flames.

In the north-eastern corner of the royal quarters a well of clear water appeared of itself, at which the household in amazement carried out their rites as at a holy bathing-place.

And troops of heavenly beings, petitioners for the Law, thronged the grove to wait on him, and in their wonderment they cast flowers from the trees, though out of season.

At that time the noxious creatures consorted together and did each other no hurt. Whatever diseases there were among mankind were cured too without effort.

The birds and deer did not call aloud and the rivers flowed with calm waters. The quarters became clear and the sky shone cloudless; the drums of the gods resounded in the air.

When the Guru was born for the salvation of all creatures, the world became exceeding peaceful, as though, being in a state of disorder, it had obtained a ruler. Kamadeva alone did not rejoice.

On seeing the miraculous birth of his son, the king, steadfast though he was, was much disturbed, and from his affection a double stream of tears flowed, born of delight and apprehension.

The queen was filled with fear and joy, like a stream of hot and cold water mixed, because the power of her son was other than human on the one hand, and because she had a mother's natural weakness on the other.

The pious old women failed in penetration, seeing only the reasons for alarm; so, purifying themselves and performing luck-bringing rites, they prayed to the gods for good fortune.

When the Brahmans, famed for conduct, learning and eloquence, had heard about these omens and considered them, then with beaming faces full of wonder and exultation they said to the king, who was both fearful and joyful—

"On earth men desire for their peace no excellence at all other than a son. As this lamp of yours is the lamp of your race, rejoice and make a feast to-day.

Therefore, in all steadfastness renounce anxiety and be merry; for your race will certainly nourish. He who has been born here as your son is the leader for those who are overcome by the suffering of the world.

According to the signs found on this excellent one, the brilliance of gold and the radiance of a lamp, he will certainly become either an enlightened seer or a Cakravartin monarch on earth among men.

Should he desire earthly sovereignty, then by his might and law he will stand on earth at the head of all kings, as the light of the sun at the head of all constellations.

Should he desire salvation and go to the forest, then by his knowledge and truth he will overcome all creeds and stand on the earth, like Meru king of mountains among all the heights.

As pure gold is the best of metals, Meru of mountains, the ocean of waters, the moon of planets and the sun of fires, so your son is the best of men.

His eyes gaze unwinkingly and are limpid and wide, blazing and yet mild, steady and with very long black eyelashes. How can he not have eyes that see everything ?"

Then the king said to the twice-born : "What is the cause that these excellent characteristics should be seen, as you say, in him, when they were not seen in previous great-souled kings ?" Then the Brahmans said to him —

"In respect of the wisdom, renowned deeds and fame of kings there is no question of former and latter. And, since in the nature of things there is a cause here for the effect, listen to our parallels thereto.

The science of royal policy, which neither of those seers, Bhrigu and Angiras, the founders of families, made, was created. Sire, in the course of time by their sons, Sukra and Brhaspati.

The son of Sarasvati promulgated again the lost Veda, which the men of old had not seen, and Vyasa arranged it in many sections, which Vasistha for lack of capacity had not done.

And Valmiki was the first to create the verse, which the great seer, Cyavana, did not put together, and the science of healing which Atri did not discover was later proclaimed by the seer Atreya.

And the Brahmanhood which Kusika did not win was obtained by the son of Gadhin, O king. And Sagara set a limit for the ocean which the previous descendants of Iksvaku had not fixed.

Janaka reached the position, attained by none other, of instructing the twice-bom in the methods of Yoga ; and Sura and his kin were incapable of the famous deeds of Sauri.

Therefore neither age nor family decides. Anyone may attain pre-eminence anywhere in the world; for in the case of the kings and seers the sons accomplished the various deeds their ancestors failed to do."

Thus was the king cheered and congratulated by the trustworthy twice-born, and, discharging his mind of unwelcome suspicions, he rose to a still higher degree of joy.

And in his gratification he gave with full courtesy rich gifts to the best of the twice-born, wishing that his son might become lord of the earth as prophesied and that he should not retire to the forest before reaching old age.

Then by reason of the signs and through the power of his austerities the great seer Asita learned of the birth of him who was to put an end to birth, and came to the palace of the Sakya king, thirsting for the holy Law.

He was the chief among the knowers of the Absolute and shone with the majesty of priestly power and with the majesty of asceticism. Accordingly the king's spiritual director brought him into the regal palace with reverence and honour.

He entered the precincts of the royal women's dwelling and the rush of joy that he felt was occasioned only by the birth of the prince; for from the intensity of his austerities and the support afforded by old age he remained otherwise unmoved, deeming himself to be, as it were, in a forest.

Then the king rightly honoured the sage, when seated, with water for the feet and the proper offerings, and then addressed him with due courtesy, as Antideva of old did Vasistha—

"Fortunate am I and honoured this house that Your Holiness should deign to visit me. Be pleased to command what I should do, O benign one: I am your disciple and you should show confidence in me."

When the sage was invited in this befitting fashion by the king with all cordiality, his large eyes opened wide in admiration and he spoke these profound and solemn words :—

"It indeed accords with your great soul, your hospitality, your generosity, your piety, that you should thus show to me a kindly disposition, so worthy of your nature, family, wisdom and age.

And this is the course by which those royal seers, acquiring wealth by the subtle Law, ever continued giving it away according to rule, thus being rich in austerities and poor in worldly goods.

But hear the reason for my visit and be rejoiced.

In the path of the sun I heard a divine voice saying, "To thee is born a son for Enlightenment."

As soon as I heard the voice, I put my mind into trance and understood the matter through the signs. Then I came here to see the lofty banner of the Sakya race uplifted like the banner of Indra."

When the king heard him speak thus, his bearing was disordered with delight, and he took the prince, as he lay on his nurse's lap, and showed him to the ascetic.

Then the great seer wonderingly beheld the prince, the soles of his feet marked with a wheel, the fingers and toes joined by a web, the circle of hair growing between his eye-brows and the testicles withdrawn like an elephant's.

And when he saw him resting on the nurse's lap, like the son of Agni on Devi's lap, tears flickered on his eyelashes and, sighing, he looked up to heaven.

But when the king saw Asita's eyes swimming with tears, he trembled from affection for his son, and sobbing with his throat choked with weeping, he clasped his hands and bowed his body, asking him—

"Why are you, who are so steadfast, tearful on seeing him who differs little in form from the gods, whose brilliant birth has been attended by many miracles and whose future lot you say is to be the highest ?

Will the prince be long-lived. Holy One ? Surely he is not born for my sorrow ? Shall the two handfuls of water been obtained by me with such difficulty, only for Death to come and drink them up ?

Is the treasure of my fame inexhaustible ? Is the dominion to last for ever in the hands of my family ? Shall I win bliss in the next world, even in the sleep of death having one eye open in the shape of my son ?

Is this young shoot of my family, just sprung up, fated to wither without flowering ? Tell me quickly, Lord, I am all uneasy; for you know the love of fathers for their sons."

The seer understood how the king was troubled by the thought of misfortune and said: "Let not your mind, O king, be disturbed; what I have said is not open to doubt.

My agitation is not over aught untoward for him, but I am distressed for my own disappointment. For my time to depart has come, just when he is born—who shall understand the means, so hard to find, of destroying birth.

For he will give up the kingdom in his indifference to worldly pleasures, and, through bitter struggles grasping the final truth, he will shine forth as a sun of knowledge in the world to dispel the darkness of delusion.

With the mighty boat of knowledge he will bring the world, which is being carried away in affliction, up from the ocean of suffering, which is overspread with the foam of disease and which has old age for its waves and death for its fearsome flood.

The world of the living, oppressed with the thirst of desires, will drink the flowing stream of his most excellent Law, which is cooled by concentration of thought and has mystic wisdom for the current of its water, firm discipline for its banks and vows for its Brahminy ducks.

For to those who, finding themselves on the desert-tracks of the cycle of existence, are harassed by suffering and obstructed by the objects of sense, he will proclaim the way of salvation, as to travellers who have lost their road.

Like a mighty cloud with its rain at the close of the summer heat, he will give relief with the rain of the Law to men burnt up in the world with the fire of the passions, whose fuel is the objects of sense.

With the most excellent irresistible key of the good Law he will throw open for the escape of living beings the door whose bolt is the thirst of desire and whose leaves are delusion and the darkness of ignorance.

And, as king of the Law, he will reach Enlightenment and release from prison the world which is entangled in its own snares of delusion and which is overwhelmed by suffering and destitute of refuge.

Therefore be not grieved for him; in this living world that man is to be deplored who through delusion, by reason of the sensual pleasures or through intoxication of mind, refuses to hear the final, Law.

Therefore, though I have obtained the trances, I have not won through to the goal, in that I have fallen short of this merit. For, since I shall not hear his Law, I hold even rebirth in the triple heaven to be a disaster."

Hearing this explanation, the -king with his queen and friends was quit of his dejection and rejoiced ; for he deemed it to be his own good fortune that his son should be such.

But his heart busied itself anxiously with the thought that his son would follow the path of the sages. It was most certainly not that he was opposed to the side of the Law, but that he saw the danger arising from failure of issue.

Then when the seer, Asita, had made known the truth about his son to the king who was troubled about him, he departed, as he had come, by the path of the wind, while they looked up at him with all reverence.

Then the saint, who had attained right knowledge, saw his younger sister's son and straitly charged him in his compassion, as if he were his own dear son, to listen to the words of the Sage and to follow his teaching.

The king too, delighted at the birth of a son, threw open all the prisons in his realm and in his affection for his son caused the birth ceremony to be properly performed for him in the manner that befitted his family.

And, when the ten days were fulfilled, in the piety of his mind and the excess of his joy, he offered for the supreme welfare of his son sacrifices to the gods together with incantations, oblations and other auspicious rites.

Moreover for the prosperity of his son he bestowed of himself cows full of milk, in the prime of their age, with gilded horns and healthy sturdy calves, to the full number of a hundred thousand, on the twice-born.

Thereon, self-controlled, he prescribed the performance of ceremonies directed to many ends which delighted his heart, and when a fortunate, auspicious day had been determined, he gladly decided to enter the city.

Then the queen, taking the babe, did obeisance to the gods and entered for good fortune a costly ivory litter, bedecked with white *sitapuspa* flowers and lit by precious stones.

The king then made the queen, attended by aged women and accompanied by her child, enter the city in front of him, and himself also advanced, saluted by hosts of citizens, like

Indra, when on entering heaven he was saluted by the immortals.

The Sakya king thereon proceeded into his palace in good heart, like Bhava on the birth of his six-faced son, and, with countenance beaming with joy, directed every arrangement to be made which would lead to many kinds of prosperity and renown.

Thus the town named after Kapila rejoiced with its surrounding territory at the prosperous birth of the prince, just as the town of the Wealth-giver, which was thronged with Apsarases, rejoiced at the birth of Nalakubara.

2

LIFE IN THE PALACE

Day by day from the birth of his son, the master of self, who had come to the end of birth and old age, the king waxed mightier in riches, elephants, horses and allies, as a river waxes with the inflow of waters.

For then he obtained many treasures of wealth and jewels of every kind and of gold, wrought and unwrought, so as to overload even that chariot of the mind, desire.

And rut-maddened elephants from the Himalayas, such as even lords of elephants like Padma could not have brought to his stables in this world, served him, and that too without any effort on his part.

And his city shook with the tread of horses, adorned with the various marks and decked with trappings of fresh gold, or laden with ornaments and having flowing manes, which he acquired either through his military power, from his allies, or by purchase.

And so too there were in his kingdom many excellent cows, contented and well-nourished, unspotted, giving pure and abundant milk, and accompanied by well-grown calves.

His enemies became neutrals, neutrality turned into alliance, allies were united to him with peculiar firmness. He had only two parties; but the third, enemies, did not exist.

So too for him heaven rained in due time and place, with gentle winds and rumbling clouds, and with the sky adorned with rings of lightning, but without the evils of showers of thunderbolts or falls of meteoric stones.

At that time fruitful grain grew according to season,

even without the labour of tilling; and the very herbs for him became still more abounding in juice and substance.

Though that hour brings as much danger to the body as the clash of armies, yet women were delivered in due time safely, easily and without disease.

Except for those who had taken vows of mendicancy, no one begged from others, however wretched his means might be; and at that time no man of position, poverty-stricken though he were, turned his face away when solicited.

At that time in his realm, as in that of king Yayati the son of Nahusa, no one was disrespectful to his elders, or lacking in generosity, or irreligious, or deceitful, or given to hurt.

And by constructing there gardens, temples, hermitages, wells, water-halls, lotus-ponds and groves, they showed their devotion to *dharma*, as if they had seen Paradise before their eyes.

And in the joy of deliverance from famine, peril and disease, the people were as happy as in Paradise. Husband did not transgress against wife, nor wife against husband.

None pursued love for sensual pleasure; none withheld wealth from others to gratify his own desires; none practised religion for the sake of riches; none did hurt on the plea of religion.

Theft and the like and enmity disappeared. His kingdom was at ease and independent, free from foreign rule, peaceful and prosperous, like the kingdom of Anaranya of old.

For then at the prince's birth in the realm of that king, as in that of Manu, son of the Sun, joy prevailed, evil perished, *dharma* blazed forth, sin was quenched.

Since the prosperity of the royal race and the accomplishment of all objects had been thus brought to pass, the king named his son accordingly, saying "He is Sarvarthasiddha".

But when queen Maya saw the vast power of her son, like that of a divine seer, she was unable to bear the joy it caused her; then she went to Heaven to dwell there.

Then the queen's sister, who equalled her in majesty and did not fall below her in affection and tenderness, brought up the prince, who was like a scion of the gods, as if he were her own son.

Then the prince gradually grew up in all due perfection, like the young sun on the Eastern mountain, or the flame fanned by the wind, or the lord of the stars in the bright fortnight.

Then they brought to him from the houses of his friends priceless unguents of sandalwood and strings of jewels, filled with magic herbs, and little golden carts to which deer were harnessed, and ornaments suited to his age and little elephants, deer and horses of gold, and chariots yoked with little oxen, and dolls gay with gold and silver.

Though but a child and attended in this fashion by the various kinds of sensory pleasure suitable to his age, yet in gravity, purity, thoughtfulness and dignity he was unlike a child.

He passed through infancy and in course of time duly underwent the ceremony of initiation. And it took him but a few days to learn the sciences suitable to his race, the mastery of which ordinarily requires many years.

But, as the king of the Sakyas had heard from the great seer, Asita, that the prince's future goal would be the supreme beatitude, he feared lest he should go to the forests and therefore he turned him to sensual pleasures.

Then from a family possessed of long-standing good conduct he summoned for him the goddess of Fortune in the shape of a maiden, Yasodhara by name, of widespread renown, virtuous and endowed with beauty, modesty and gentle bearing.

The prince, radiant with wondrous beauty like Sanatkumara, took his delight with the Sakya king's daughter-in-law, as the Thousand-eyed with Saci.

The monarch, reflecting that the prince must see nothing untoward that might agitate his mind, assigned him a dwelling in the upper storey of the palace and did not allow him access to the ground.

Then in the pavilions, white as the clouds of autumn, with apartments suited to each season and resembling heavenly mansions come down to earth, he passed the time with the noble music of singing-women.

For the palace was glorious as Kailasa, with tambourines whose frames were bound with gold and which sounded softly beneath the strokes of women's fingers, and with dances that rivalled those of the beautiful Apsarases.

There the women delighted him with their soft voices, charming blandishments, playful intoxications, sweet laughter, curvings of eyebrows and sidelong glances.

Then, a captive to the women, who were skilled in the accessories of love and indefatigable in sexual pleasure, he did not descend from the palace to the ground, just as one who has won Paradise by his merit does not descend to earth from the heavenly mansion.

But the king, for the sake of his son'a prosperity and spurred on by the goal predicted for him, abode in holy peace, desisted from sin, practised self-restraint and rewarded the good.

He did not, like one wanting in self-control, indulge in the pleasures of the senses; he cherished no improper passion for women; with firmness he overcame the rebellious horses of the senses, and conquered his kinsmen and subjects by his virtues.

He did not learn science to cause suffering to others, but studied only the knowledge that was beneficent; for he wished well to all people as much as to his own subjects.

And for the long life of his son he worshipped the shining constellation, whose regent is Brhaspati, and he offered oblations in a huge fire and presented the twice-born with gold and cattle.

He bathed to purify his body with the waters of the sacred bathing-places and his mind with the waters of the virtues, and at the same time he drank *soma* as enjoined by the Vedas and observed in his heart the self-produced bliss of religious tranquillity.

He spoke what was pleasant and not unprofitable; he stated what was true and not disagreeable; for self-respect made him unable to say even to himself a pleasant falsehood or a harsh truth.

He gave no opening, to feelings of partiality or the reverse, according as he liked or disliked his petitioners, and observed purity of justice as being holy; for he did not esteem sacrifice to be so in the same degree.

He ever quenched straightway with the water of gifts the thirst of expectant suppliants, and with the battle-axe of good conduct, instead of by fighting, he broke down the swollen pride of his foes.

He disciplined the one; he protected the seven; seven too he abandoned and he observed five; he won the set of three; he understood the set of three; he knew the set of two and gave up the set of two.

He did not have the guilty executed, although he adjudged them worthy of death, nor did he even regard them with anger. And he inflicted mild punishments on them, since their release too was looked on as bad policy.

He carried out the most difficult vows of the ancient seers; he gave up long-cherished feuds, and he obtained renown, made fragrant by virtue; he swept away the dust of defiling passions.

He did not desire to exact revenue beyond the amount due, he had no wish to covet the goods of others. And he did not desire to expose the wickedness of his adversaries, nor did he wish to bear wrath in his heart.

Since the monarch behaved thus, his servants and the citizens followed the same course, just as, when the mind of a man in mystic trance has become wholly calm and is compact of tranquillity, his senses become so likewise.

Then in the course of time the fair-bosomed Yasodhara, bearing her own fame, bore to the son of Suddhodana a son, Rahula by name, with the face of Rahu's adversary.

Then the ruler of the earth, in possession of the son he had longed for and fully assured of the prosperity of his race, rejoiced at the birth of a grandson as much as he had rejoiced at the birth of a son.

Overjoyed at the thought that his son would feel paternal affection, just as he himself felt it, he attended to the various ceremonies at the proper season, as if in his love for his son he were on the point of mounting to Paradise.

Abiding in the path of the great kings of the golden age, he practised austerities without even doffing the white garments of ordinary life and worshipped with sacrifices that brought no injury to living creatures.

Then by his good merit he shone forth gloriously with the splendour of sovereignty and of asceticism alike and was illumined by his family, conduct and wisdom, wishing to diffuse brightness like the thousand-rayed sun.

And he, whose sovereignty was established, honoured and intoned the holy chants of Svayambhu and performed works of great difficulty, like Ka in the primeval age when he wished to produce creatures.

He laid aside weapons, he pondered on the *Sastra,* he pursued holy calm, he undertook the law of restraint; like one who is self-controlled, he was not a slave to any object of sense; he looked like a father on all his domains.

For he maintained the kingdom for the sake of his son, his son for his family and his family for his renown, his fame for heaven, heaven for the sake of his self; he only desired the continuance of his self for the sake of *dharma.*

Thus he performed the manifold *dharma,* which is observed by the religious and is established through revelation, ever hoping that, now that the prince had seen the face of his son, he would not go to the forest.

Kings who in this world desire to preserve their personal sovereignty guard their sons, but this *dharma*-loving lord of men by letting his son loose among the objects of sense kept him from *dharma.*

But all the Bodhisattvas, those beings of incomparable natures, first tasted the flavour of worldly pleasures and then, when a son was born to them, left for the forest. Hence, though the motive cause was fully developed in him by the accumulation of past acts, he enjoyed sensual pleasure till he reached Illumination.

3

THE PRINCE's PERTURBATION

Then upon a time he listened to songs celebrating the forests, with their soft grass, with their trees resounding with koils' calls, and with their adornment of lotusponds.

Then hearing of the entrancing character of the city groves, beloved of the womenfolk, he set his heart on an expedition outside, like an elephant confined inside a house.

Then the king learnt of the state of mind of that heart's desire, styled his son, and directed a pleasure excursion to be prepared worthy of his love and majesty and of his son's youth.

And, reflecting that the prince's tender mind might be perturbed thereby, he forbade the appearance of afflicted common folk on the royal road.

Then with the greatest gentleness they cleared away on all sides those whose limbs were maimed or senses defective, the aged, sick and the like, and the wretched, and made the royal highway supremely magnificent.

Then, when the road had been made beautiful, the prince, after receiving permission, descended at the proper time in full splendour with well-trained attendants from the top of the palace, and approached the king.

Thereon the ruler of men, with tears in his eyes, gazed long at his son and kissed him on the head ; and with his voice he bade him set forth, but out of affection he did not let him go in his mind.

Then the prince mounted a golden chariot, to which were harnessed four well-broken horses with golden gear, and with a driver who was manly, skilful and reliable.

Then, like the moon with the constellations mounting to the sky, he proceeded with a suitable retinue towards the road which was bestrewn with heaps of brilliant flowers and made gay with hanging wreaths and fluttering banners.

And very slowly he entered the royal highway, which was carpeted with the halves of blue lotuses in the shape of eyes open to their widest in excitement, as all around the citizens gazed at him.

Some praised him for his gracious bearing, others worshipped him for his glorious appearance, but for his benignity others wished him sovereignty and length of days.

From the great houses humpbacks and swarms of dwarfs and Kiratas poured forth, and from the meaner houses women; and all bowed down as to the flag in the procession of the god.

Hearing the news from their servants, " the prince, they say, is going out", the women obtained leave from their elders and went out on to the balconies in their desire to see him.

They gathered together in uncontrollable excitement, obstructed by the slipping of their girdle-strings, as they put their ornaments on at the report, and with their eyes still dazed by sudden awakening from sleep.

They frightened the flocks of birds on the houses with the jingling of zones, the tinkling of anklets and the clatter of their steps on the stairs, and reproached each other for jostling.

But some of these magnificent women, though longing made them try to rush, were delayed in their movements by the weight of their chariot-like hips and full breasts.

But another, though well able to move with speed, checked her steps and went slowly, modestly shrinking as she covered up the ornaments worn in intimacy.

Unquiet reigned in the windows then, as the women were crowded together in the mutual press, with their earrings ever agitated by collisions and their ornaments jingling.

But the lotus-faces of the women, emerging from the windows and mutually setting their earrings in perpetual commotion, seemed like lotuses stuck on to the pavilions.

Then with its palaces full to bursting with young women, who threw the lattices open in their excitement, the city appeared as magnificent on all sides as Paradise with its heavenly mansions full of Apsarases.

From the narrowness of the windows the faces of these glorious women, with their earrings resting on each other's cheeks, seemed like bunches of lotus-flowers tied to the windows.

The, women, looking down at the prince in the street, seemed as if wishing to descend to earth, while the men, gazing up at him with upraised faces, seemed as if wishing to rise to heaven.

Beholding the king's son in the full glory of his beauty and majesty, the women murmured low, "Blessed is his wife", with pure minds and from no baser motive;

For they held him in reverent awe, reflecting that he with the long stout arms, in form like the visible presence of the god whose symbols are flowers, would, it was said, resign his royal pomp and follow the religious law.

Thus the first time that the prince saw the royal highway, it was thronged with respectful citizens, clad in cleanly sober guise; and he rejoiced and felt in some degree as if he were being re-created.

But when the Suddhadhivasa gods saw that city as joyful as Paradise itself, they created the illusion of an old man in order to incite the king's son to leave his home.

Then the prince saw him overcome with senility and different in form to other men. His interest was excited and, with gaze steadily directed on the man, he asked the charioteer—

"Good charioteer, who is this man with white hair, supporting himself on the staff in his hand, with his eyes veiled by the brows, and limbs relaxed and bent ? Is this some transformation in him, or his original state, or mere chance ?"

When the chariot-driver was thus spoken to, those very same gods confounded his understanding, so that, without seeing his error, he told the prince the matter he should have withheld:—

"Old age it is called, that which has broken him down—the murderer of beauty, the ruin of vigour, the birthplace of sorrow, the grave of pleasure, the destroyer of memory, the enemy of the senses.

For he too sucked milk in his infancy, and later in course of time he crawled on the ground; in the natural order he became a handsome youth and in the same natural order he has now reached old age."

At these words the king's son started a little and addressed the charioteer thus, "Will this evil come upon me also ?" Then the charioteer said to him:—

"Inevitably by force of time my long-lived lord will know this length of his days. Men are aware that old age thus destroys beauty and yet they seek it."

Then, since his mind was purified by his intentions in the past and his good merit had been accumulated through countless epochs, he was perturbed in his lofty soul at hearing of old age, like a bull on hearing the crash of a thunderbolt near by.

Fixing his eye on the old man, he sighed deeply and shook his head; and looking on the festive multitude he uttered these words in his perturbation:—

"Thus old age strikes down indiscriminately memory and beauty and valour, and yet with such a sight before its eyes the world is not perturbed.

This being so, turn back the horses, charioteer; go quickly home again. For how can I take my pleasure in the garden, when the fear of old age rules in my mind ?"

So at the bidding of his master's son the driver turned back the chariot. Then the prince returned to the same palace, but so lost in anxiety that it seemed to him empty.

But even there he found no relief, as he ever dwelt on the subject of old age; therefore once more with the permission of the king he went out, all being ordered as before.

Thereupon the same gods created a man with body afflicted by disease, and the son of Suddhodana saw him, and, keeping his gaze fixed on him, he said to the charioteer:—

"Who is this man with swollen belly and body that

heaves with his panting ? His shoulders and arms are fallen in, his limbs emaciated and pale. He calls out piteously, "mother", as he leans on another for support."

Then the charioteer replied to him," Good Sir, it is the mighty misfortune called disease, developed in full force from the disorder of the humours, that has made this man, once so competent, no longer master of himself".

Thereupon the king's son looked at the man compassionately and spoke, "Is this evil peculiar to him, or is the danger of disease common to all men?"

Then.the chariot-driver said, "Prince, this evil is shared by all. For men feast and yet they are thus oppressed by disease and racked by pain."

Hearing this truth, he was perturbed in mind and trembled like the reflection of the moon on rippling water; and in his pity he uttered these words in a somewhat low tone:—

"This is the calamity of disease for mankind and yet the world sees it and feels no alarm. Vast, alas, is the ignorance of men, who sport under the very shadow of disease.

Turn back the chariot, charioteer, from going outside; let it go straight to the palace of the chief of men. And on hearing of the danger of disease, my mind is repelled from pleasures and shrinks, as it were, into itself."

Then he turned back with all feeling of joy gone and entered the palace, given over to brooding; and seeing him thus returned a second time, the lord of the earth made enquiry.

But when he learnt the reason for his return, he felt himself already abandoned by him. And he merely reprimanded the officer in charge of clearing the road, and angry though he was, imposed no severe punishment on him.

And he further arranged for his son the application of sensual attractions in the highest degree, hoping, "Perhaps he will be held by the restlessness of the senses and not desert us".

But when in the women's apartments his son took no pleasure in the objects of sense, sounds and the rest, then he directed another excursion outside with the thought that it might cause a change of mood.

And as out of his affection he understood his son's state of mind and took no account of the dangers of passion, he ordered suitable courtesans to be present there, as skilled in the arts.

Then the royal highway was decorated and guarded with especial care; and the king changed the charioteer and chariot and sent the prince off outside.

Then as the king's son was going along, those same gods fashioned a lifeless man, so that only the charioteer and the prince, and none other, saw the corpse being borne along.

Thereon the king's son asked the charioteer, "Who is being carried along yonder by four men and followed by a dejected company ? He is dressed out gorgeously and yet they bewail him".

Then the driver's mind was overcome by the pure-natured Suddhadhivasa gods and, though it should not have been told, he explained this matter to the lord of mankind:—

"This is someone or other, lying bereft of intellect, senses, breath and qualities, unconscious and become like a mere log or bundle of grass. He was brought up and cherished most lovingly with every care and now he is being abandoned."

Hearing the driver's reply, he was slightly startled and said, "Is this law of being peculiar to this man, or is such the end of all creatures ?"

Then the driver said to him, "This is the last act for all creatures. Destruction is inevitable for all in the world, be he of low or middle or high degree".

Then, steadfast-minded though he was, the king's son suddenly became faint on hearing of death, and, leaning with his shoulder against the top of the chariot rail, he said in a melodious voice :—

"This is the end appointed for all creatures, and yet the world throws off fear and takes no heed. Hardened, I ween, are men's hearts ; for they are in good cheer, as they fare along the road.

Therefore, charioteer, let our chariot be turned back; for it is not the time or place for pleasure-resorts. For how could a man of intelligence be heedless here in the hour of calamity, when once he knows of destruction ?"

Though the king's son spoke to him thus, he not merely did not turn back but in accordance with the king's command went on to the Padmasanda grove, which had been provided with special attractions.

There the prince saw that lovely grove like the grove of Nandana, with young trees in full bloom, with intoxicated koils flitting joyously about, and with pavilions and tanks beautiful with lotuses.

Then the king's son was carried off by force to that grove, crowded with troops of beautiful women, and was afraid of obstacles to the religious life like some anchorite novice conveyed by force to the palace of the monarch of Alaka, filled with glorious Apsarases.

4

THE WOMEN-REJECTION

Then the women went forth from the city garden, their eyes dancing with excitement, to meet the king's son, as if he were a bridegroom arriving.

And, as they approached him, their eyes opened wide in wonder and they welcomed him respectfully with hands folded like lotus-buds.

And they stood around him, their minds absorbed in love, and seemed to drink him in with eyes that were moveless and blossomed wide in ecstasy.

For the glory of the brilliant signs on his person, as of ornaments born on him, made the women deem him to be the god of love in bodily form.

Some opined from his benignity and gravity that the moon had come down to earth in person with his rays veiled.

Enthralled by his beauty, they writhed suppressedly, and, smiting each other with their glances, softly sighed.

Thus the women did no more than gaze at him with their eyes and were *so* constrained by his power, that they neither uttered anything nor laughed.

But the purohita's son, the sagacious Udayin, seeing them to be so embarrassed by love as to be attempting nothing, addressed these words to them:—

"You are all of you skilled in all the arts, adepts at captivating the feelings, possessed of beauty and charm, and pre-eminent in your endowments.

With these gifts you would even grace the Northern Kurus and the pleasaunce of Kubera, much more then this earth.

You could make even lust-free seers waver, and captivate even gods who are accustomed to the Apsarases.

And by your knowledge of the sentiments, your blandishments, your wealth of charm and beauty, you have power over women, how much more then over men in respect of passion?

When with such qualities you are lax, each of you, in your own special accomplishment, and exhibit such conduct, I am displeased with your simplicity.

Conduct such as this of yours would be more proper in brides who narrow their eyes in shame, or even in the wives of cowherds.

As for the argument that he is steadfast and exalted by the power of his majesty, after all the might of women is great; therefore show determination in this matter.

Of old time, for instance, the great .seer, Vyasa, whom even the gods could hardly contend with, was kicked with her foot by the harlot, Kasisundari.

Manthala Gautama, desirous of intercourse with the courtesan, Jangha, and wishful of pleasing her, of old carried forth dead bodies with that end in view.

A young woman, low in caste and standing, gratified the heart of the great seer, Dirghatapas Gautama, when he was old in years.

Similarly the sage's son, Rsyasrnga, who had no knowledge of women, was entrapped and borne off by Santa with various wiles.

And the great seer, Visvamitra, though he had entered on mighty austerities, was captivated by the Apsaras, Ghrtaoi, and deemed ten years with her but a day.

To many such seers as these have women brought emotion ; how much more then can they to the innocent son of a king in the flower of his youth ?

This being so, exert yourselves boldly, so that the good fortune of the king's family may not turn away from here.

23. For ordinary women captivate lovers of the same class as themselves; but they only are truly women who ensnare the feelings of high and low alike."

On hearing these words of Udayin, the damsels were so to speak cut to the heart and set themselves to the task of capturing the prince.

As if somewhat frightened, the women made gestures designed to cause rapture with brows, looks and blandishments, with laughter, frolicking and movements.

But what with the king's command, and the prince's gentleness and the power of intoxication and love, they soon abandoned timidity.

Then surrounded by the women, the prince wandered through the garden, like an elephant through the Himalayan forest, accompanied by a heard of feales.

In that lovely grove he shone with the women in attendance on him, like Vivasvat surrounded by Apsarases in the pleasaunce of Vibhraja.

Then some of the young women there, pretending to be under the influence of intoxication, touched him with thier firm, rounded, close-set, charming breasts.

One made a false stumble and clasped him by force with her tender arm-creepers, which hung down loosely from her drooping shoulders.

Another, whose mouth with copper-coloured lower lip smelt of spirituous liquor, whispered in his ear, "Listen to a secret."

Another, who was all wet with unguents, said as if commanding him, "Make a line here", in the hope of winning the touch of his hand.

Another repeatedly let her blue garments slip down under the pretext of intoxication, and with her girdle partly seen she seemed like the night with the lightning flashing.

Some walked up and down so as to make their golden zones tinkle and displayed to him their hips veiled by diaphanous robes.

Others grasped mango-boughs in full flower and leaned so as to display bosoms like golden jars.

Another lotus-eyed damsel came from a lotus-bed with a lotus and stood by the side of the lotus-faced prince as if she were Padmasri.

Another sang a sweet song with gesticulations to bring out the sense, reproving his indifference, as it were, with looks that said, "You deceive yourself".

Another imitated him by drawing the bow of her brows on her fair countenance and making gestures in mimicry of his solemnity.

A damsel with fine rounded breasts and earrings shaking with her laughter mocked him out loud, saying, "Finish it. Sir".

Similarly, as he was retreating, some bound him with ropes of garlands, and others restrained him with words that were like ankuses but were softened with innuendoes.

Another in order to bring about an argument seized a mango-spray and asked, stuttering with intoxication, "Whose flower now is this ? "

One of them, modelling her gait and outward appearance on those of a man, said to him, "Sir, you have been conquered by women, conquer this earth now !"

Then another with rolling eyes sniffed at a blue lotus and addressed the prince with words that were slightly indistinct in her excitement:—

" See, my lord, this mango loaded with honey-scented flowers, in which the koil calls, looking as if imprisoned in a golden cage.

Look at this *asoka* tree, the increaser of lovers' sorrows, in which the bees murmur as if scorched by fire.

Behold this *tilaka* tree, embraced by a mango branch, like a man in white garments embraced by a woman with yellow body-paint.

See the *kurubaka* in full bloom, shining like lac just squeezed out, which bends over as if dazzled by the brilliance of the women's nails.

And look at this young *asoka* tree, all covered with young shoots, which stands as if abashed by the glitter of our hands.

See the pond enveloped by the *sinduvara* bushes growing on its bank, like a woman lying down and clothed in white silk.

Consider the mighty power of women; for instance, the sheldrake in the water there follows obediently behind his mate like a servant.

Listen to the sound of the impassioned cuckoo's cry; another koil calls at once like an echo.

Can it be that spring brings passion to the birds, but not to the wiseacre who reflects on what he should not reflect on ?"

Thus these young women, to whose minds love had given free rein, assailed the prince with wiles of every kind.

But despite such allurements the prince firmly guarded his senses, and in his perturbation over the inevitability of death, was neither rejoiced nor distressed.

He, the supreme man, saw that they had no firm footing in the real truth, and with mind that was at the same time both perturbed and steadfast he thus meditated:—

"Do these women then not understand the transitoriness of youth, that they are so inebriated with their own beauty, which old age will destroy ?

Surely they do not perceive anyone overwhelmed by illness, that they are so full of mirth, so void of fear in a world in which disease is a law of nature.

And quite clearly they sport and laugh so much at ease and unperturbed, because they are ignorant of death who carries all away.

For what rational being would stand or sit or lie at ease, still less laugh, when he knows of old age, disease and death ?

But he is just like a being without reason, who, on seeing another aged or ill or even dead, remains indifferent and unmoved.

For when one tree is shorn both of its flowers and its fruit and falls or is cut down, another tree is not distressed thereby."

Then Udayin, who was expert in worldly conduct and the *sastras,* seeing him to be absorbed in brooding and to have lost all desire for sensual objects, addressed him thus out of friendship :—

"The king appointed me to be your companion because he considered me competent; therefore I wish to speak to you to justify the confidence he reposed in me.

The threefold characteristic of friendship is to restrain a man from what is unprofitable, to encourage him to what is profitable and to stand by him in adversity.

If, after having promised friendship, I should resile from the duty of a man and neglect your interests, there would be no friendship in me.

Therefore, having become your friend, I say that such lack of courtesy to women ill befits one who is as young in years and beautiful in person as you are.

The gratification of women, even by the use of falsity, is right, for the sake both of countering their bashfulness and of one's own enjoyment.

It is humility and compliance that bind women's hearts; for good qualities are the birthplace of affection and women like respect.

Therefore, O large-eyed prince, however averse your heart be, you should gratify them with a courtesy that corresponds to this beauty of yours.

Courtesy is the balm of women, courtesy is the best ornament; beauty without courtesy is like a grove without flowers.

What is the good of courtesy only ? Accept them with genuine feeling. For when you have obtained such rare pleasures of the senses, you should not contemn them.

Knowing that love is the highest good, even the god, Puramdara, for instance, of olden time fell in love with Ahalya, the wife of Gautama.

And according to tradition Agastya asked for Rohini, wife of Soma, and thereby obtained Lopamudra who resembled her.

And Brhaspati of the great austerities begot Bharadvaja on Mamata, the Maruti, wife of Utathya.

And the Moon, the best of sacrificers, begot Budha of the god-like deeds on Brhaspati's wife, as she was making oblations.

And of old too Parasara, with his passions inflamed, approached Kali, the daughter of a fish, on the bank of the Yamuna.

The sage Vasistha through lust begot a son, Kapinjalada, on a despised low-caste woman, Aksamala.

And the royal seer, Yayati, even when his term of life had run out, dallied with the Apsaras, Visvaci, in the Caitraratha grove.

And though the Kaurava king, Pandu, knew that intercourse with a woman must end in his death, yet, allured by Madri's entrancing beauty, he gave himself up to the pleasures of love.

And Karalajanaka too carried off a Brahman's daughter, and, though he thus incurred ruin, he still adhered to his love.

Men of lofty position such as these for the sake of sexual pleasure enjoyed the objects of the senses, even contemptible ones, and all the more so when they were conjoined with excellence.

You, however, who possess vigour, beauty and youth, despise the pleasures which have come to you of right, and to which the world is attached."

The prince listened to his specious words, supported by scriptural tradition, and replied to him in a voice like the thundering of a cloud :—

"Your words make plain your friendship for me and befit you; and I shall satisfy you on the points wherein you misjudge me.

It is not that I despise the objects of sense and I know that the world is devoted to them; but my mind does not delight in them, because I hold them to be transitory.

If the triad of old age, disease and death did not exist, I too should take my pleasure in the ravishing objects of sense.

For if indeed this beauty of women could have been rendered everlasting, my mind would certainly have taken pleasure in the passions, full of evils though they are.

But seeing that, when their beauty has been drunk up by old age, it will be abhorrent even to them, delight in it could only arise from delusion.

For a man who, himself subject to death, disease and old age, sports unperturbed with those who are subject to death, disease and old age, is on a level with the birds and beasts.

As for your argument that those men of might were addicted to passion, that rather must cause perturbation of mind, seeing that they too perished.

And I do not hold that to be true greatness, which has the generic characteristic of perishing, and in which either there is attachment to the objects of sense, or self-control is not attained.

As for your saying that one should associate with women, even by the use of falsity, I cannot reconcile falsity with courtesy by any means at all.

Nor does that compliance please me, from which straightforwardness is absent. Fie upon that union, which is not made wholeheartedly!

For ought one to deceive a soul inflamed with passion, which is lacking in steadfastness, trusting, attached, and blind to the dangers incurred?

And surely it is not fit for women to look at men or men at women, when the victims of passion one for the other, if they practise deceit in this way.

Such being the case, you should not lead me astray to the ignoble passions, when I am afflicted with suffering and my lot is old age and death.

Ah! Your mind must be very firm and strong, when you find substance in the fleeting passions. While observing creation on the road of death, you remain attached to the objects of sense in the midst of the most terrible danger.

I on the other hand am fearful and exceeding distressed, as I meditate on the terrors of old age, death and disease. I find no peace or contentment, much less pleasure, as I perceive the world blazing as it were with fire.

If desire arises in the heart of a man who knows that death is inevitable, I consider that his soul is made of iron, in that instead of weeping he delights in the great danger."

Then, as the prince uttered this discourse which was full of resolution and controverted recourse to the passions, the lord of day passed to the Western Mountain, with his orb such that men could gaze at it.

Then their garlands and ornaments worn in vain, their excellent arts and endearments all fruitless, the women suppressed the god of love in his birthplace, their hearts, and returned to the city with their hopes frustrated.

Then the son of earth's guardian saw the glory of the women in the city garden withdrawn again in the evening and, meditating on the transitoriness of everything, he entered his dwelling.

But when the king heard that his son was averse from the objects of sense, then like an elephant with a dart in its heart, he did not lie down that night. Thereon wearing himself out with all kinds of counsels with his ministers, he found no means, other than the passions, for restraining his son's purpose.

5

FLIGHT

Though the son of the Sakya king was thus tempted by priceless objects of sense, he felt no contentment, he obtained no relief, like a lion pierced deeply in the heart by a poisoned arrow.

Then longing for spiritual peace, he set forth outside with the king's permission in order to see the forest, and for companions he had a retinue of ministers' sons, chosen for their reliability and skill in converse.

He went out, mounted on the good horse Kanthaka, the bells of whose bit were of fresh gold and whose golden trappings were beautified with waving chowries, and so he resembled a *karnikdra* emblem mounted on a flagpole.

Desire for the forest as well as the excellence of the land led him on to the more distant jungle-land, and he saw the soil being ploughed, with its surface broken with the tracks of the furrows like waves of water.

When he saw the ground in this state, with the young grass torn up and scattered by the ploughs and littered with dead worms, insects and other creatures, he mourned deeply as at the slaughter of his own kindred.

And as he observed the ploughmen with their bodies discoloured by wind, dust and the sun's rays, and the oxen in distress with the labour of drawing, the most noble one felt extreme compassion.

Then alighting from his horse, he walked slowly over the ground, overcome with grief. And as he considered the coming into being and the passing away of creation, he cried in his affliction, " How wretched this is."

And desiring to reach perfect clearness with his mind, he stopped his friends who were following him, and proceeded himself to a solitary spot at the root of a *jambu*-tree, whose beautiful leaves were waving in all directions.

And there he sat down on the clean ground, with grass bright like beryl ; and reflecting on the origin and destruction of creation he took the path of mental stillness.

And his mind at once came to a stand and at the same time he was freed from mental troubles such as desire for the objects of sense etc. And he entered into the first trance of calmness which is accompanied by gross and subtle cogitation and which is supermundane in quality.

Then he obtained possession of concentration of mind, which springs from discernment and yields extreme ecstasy and bliss, and thereafter, rightly perceiving in his mind the course of the world, he meditated on this same matter.

"A wretched thing it is indeed that man, who is himself helpless and subject to the law of old age, disease and destruction, should in his ignorance and the blindness of his conceit, pay no heed to another who is the victim of old age, disease or death.

For if I, who am myself such, should pay no heed to another whose nature is equally such, it would not be right or fitting in me, who have knowledge of this, the ultimate law."

As he thus gained correct insight into the evils of disease, old age and death, the mental intoxication relating to the self, which arises from belief in one's strength, youth and life, left him in a moment.

He did not rejoice nor yet was he downcast; doubt came not over him, nor sloth, nor drowsiness. And he felt no longing for sensual pleasures, no hatred or contempt for others.

While this pure passionless state of mind grew within his lofty soul, there came up to him a man in mendicant's clothes, unseen of other men.

The king's son asked him, "Tell me, who are you ?" On this he explained to him, "O bull among men, I am a *sramana,* who in fear of birth and death have left the home life for the sake of salvation.

Since the world is subject to destruction, I desire salvation and seek the blessed incorruptible stage. I look with equal mind on kinsman and stranger, and longing for and hatred of the objects of sense have passed from me.

I dwell wherever I happen to be, at the root of a tree or in a deserted temple, on a hill or in the forest, and I wander without ties or expectations in search of the highest good, accepting any alms I may receive."

After saying this, he flew up to the sky before the prince's very eyes; for he was a heavenly being who in that form had seen other Buddhas and had encountered him to rouse his attention.

When that being went like a bird to heaven, the best of men was thrilled and amazed. And then he gained awareness of *dharma* and set his mind on the way to leave his home.

Then he, who was Indra's peer and had conquered the horses of the senses, mounted his horse with the intention of entering the city; but out of regard for his following he did not go straight to the longed for forest.

Though he entered the city again, it was not out of any wish to do so, since he desired to make an end of old age and death and had fixed his mind in all attention on the forest life; his feelings were those of an elephant returning to the picketing-ground from the jungle.

A nobleman's daughter, looking up at him, as he entered along the road, folded her hands and said, "Happy indeed and blessed is that woman, whose husband is such in this world, O long-eyed one !"

Thereon he, whose voice was like that of a mighty thunder-cloud, heard this announcement and was filled with supreme calm. For on hearing the word "blessed", he set his mind on the means of winning final beatitude.

In stature like the peak of the golden mountain, in arm, voice and eye resembling an elephant, a thunder-cloud and a bull respectively, in countenance and step like the moon and a lion respectively, he next proceeded to the palace with yearning aroused for the imperishable *dharma*.

Then with the gait of the king of beasts he approached his father in the midst of his corps of ministers, like

Sanatkumara in the third heaven approaching Maghavat, as he shines in the assembly of the Maruts.

And prostrating himself with folded hands, he said "O king, graciously grant me permission. I wish to become a mendicant to seek salvation; for separation is inevitable for me."

Hearing his words, the king shook like a tree struck by an elephant and, grasping him by his hands folded like a lolusbud, he spoke to him thus in a voice choking with sobs—

"Refrain, dear one, from this intention. For it is not yet the time for you to give yourself up to *dharma.* For they say the practice of *dharma* in the first flush of youth, when the intelligence is still unbalanced, is full of dangers.

When a man is young with senses liable to excitement over the objects of sense and with resolution unfit to cope with the hardships of the life governed by vows, his mind shrinks back from the forest, especially so when he has had no experience of solitude.

But, O lover of *dharma,* it is now my time for *dharma,* after I have devolved the sovereignty on you, the cynosure of all eyes; but if you were forcibly to quit your father, O firmly courageous one, your *dharma* would become *non-dharma.*

Therefore give up this your resolve. Devote yourself for the present to the duties of a householder. For entry to the penance grove is agreeable to a man, after he has enjoyed the delights of youth."

Hearing these words of the king, he replied in a voice like the *kalavinka* bird's: "I will refrain from entering the penance grove, 0 king, if you will be my surety on four points.

My life is not to be subject to death. Disease is not to injure my health. Old age is not to impair my youth. Disaster is not to take away this my worldly fortune."

To his son, who had propounded a matter so hard of fulfilment, the king of the Sakyas made reply: " Give up this idea which goes too far. An extravagant wish is ridiculous and unfitting."

Then he, who was as grave as Meru is weighty, said to his father: "If this is not possible, then I am not to be stopped; for it is not right to hold back a man who wishes to escape from a house, that is being consumed by fire.

And seeing that separation is the fixed rule of the world, is it not better to make the separation myself for the sake of *dhiarma* ? Will not death sever me helplessly, still unsatisfied before I attain my goal ? "

When the lord of the earth heard this resolve of his son who was longing for salvation, he said "He shall not go", and arranged for an increased guard on him and for the choicest pleasures.

But after the ministers had duly instructed the prince according to the *sastras* with respect and candour and his father with floods of tears had stopped him from going, then he entered his dwelling in grief.

The women looked up at him with restless eyes, like young hinds, as their earrings, swinging to and fro, kissed their faces, and their bosoms heaved with uninterrupted sighs.

For, bright as the golden mountain, he bewitched the hearts of the best of women, and captivated their ears, limbs, eyes and beings with his voice, touch, beauty and qualities respectively.

As the day departed then, he mounted, blazing like the sun with his beauty, to his palace, even as the rising sun climbs Meru, in order to dispel the darkness with the splendour of his self.

Going up to a chamber which was filled with incense of the finest black aloe and had lighted candelabra glittering with gold, he repaired to a splendid golden couch inlaid with atreaka of diamond.

Then the noblest of women waited with musical instruments on him, the noblest of men, the peer of Indra, just as the troops of Apsarases wait on the son of the Lord of Wealth on the moon-white summit of Himavat.

But even those splendid instruments, though they were to the music of the gods, failed to delight or thrill him ; the one desire of the saintly prince was to leave his house in search of the bliss of the highest good, and therefore he did not rejoice.

Thereon the Akanistha deities, supreme in austerities,

taking cognisance of his resolve, all at once brought sleep there over the women and distorted the gestures of their limbs.

So one, as she lay there, supported her cheek on an unsteady hand, and, as if angry, abandoned the flute In her lap, dear though it was to her, with its decoration of gold leaf.

Another, lying with her bamboo pipe in her hands and her white robe slipping off her breasts, resembled a river with lotuses being enjoyed by a straight row of bees and with banks laughing with the foam of the water.

Similarly a third was sleeping, clasping her drum, as if it were her lover, with arms tender as the hearts of young blue lotuses, ao that the bright golden armlets had met together.

So others, decked with ornaments of freah gold, and wearing peerless yellow garments, fell down helpless with deep sleep, like *karnikara* boughs broken by an elephant.

Another lay, leaning against the side of a window with her beautiful necklaces dangling, and seemed with her slender body bent like a bow as if turned into the statue of a *sala*-plucker on a gateway.

Another again had her lotus-face bowed down, thereby causing the jewelled earrings to eat into the lines of paint, so that it took the likeness of a lotus with its stalk half-curved, as it is shaken by a *karandava* bird standing on it.

Others lay in the position in which they had sat down, and, embracing each other with intertwined arms decorated with golden bracelets, appeared to have their bodies bent down under the load of their breasts.

Yet another clasped her mighty *parivadini,* as if it were her friend, and rolled about in her sleep, so that her golden threads shook and her face had the pendent strings on her ears all disordered.

Another young woman lay, bringing her *panava,* whose beautiful netting had slipped from her armpit, between her thighs, like a lover exhausted at the end of his sport.

Others, though really large-eyed and fair-browed, showed no beauty with their eyes shut, like lotus-beds with their flowerbuds closed at the setting of the sun.

Another too had her hair loose and dishevelled, and with the ornaments and clothes fallen from her hips and her necklaces scattered she lay like an image of a woman broken by an elephant.

But others, helplessly lost to shame despite otheir natural decorum and endowment of excellent beauty, lay in immodest attitudes, snoring, and stretched their limbs, all distorted and tossing their arms about.

Others looked ugly, lying unconscious like corpses, with their ornaments and garlands cast aside, the fastening knots of their dresses undone, and eyes moveless with the whites showing.

Another lay as if sprawling in intoxication, with her mouth gaping wide, so that the saliva oozed forth, and with her limbs spread out so as to show what should have been hid. Her beauty was gone, her form distorted.

Thus these womenfolk, lying in various attitudes according to their natures, family and breeding, presented the appearance of a lotus-pond whose lotuses have been blown down and broken by the wind.

When the king's son saw the young women lying in these different ways and looking so loathsome with their uncontrolled movements, though ordinarily their forms were beautiful, their speech agreeable, he was moved to disgust:—

" Such is the real nature of woman in the world of the living, impure and loathsome ; yet man, deceived by dress and ornaments, succumbs to passion for women.

If man were to consider the natural form of woman and such a transformation produced in her by sleep, most certainly his heedlessness in respect of her would not increase; yet, overcome by his impressions of her excellence, he succumbs to passion."

Thus he recognised the difference and there arose in him a desire to escape that night. Then the gods, understanding his purpose, caused the doors of the palace to fly open.

Thereon he descended from the palace roof, condemning the women lying there, and, having descended thence, he went out unhesitatingly to the first courtyard.

He awoke the groom, the swift-footed Chandaka, and addressed him thus: "Quickly bring the horse Kanthaka; I desire to depart hence to-day to reach deathlessness.

Since contentment arises in my heart to-day, and since my resolve is fixed in my mind and since I have as it were a guide even in loneliness, most certainly the longed for goal has come into my view.

Since these women lay in my presence without regard to their own modesty or to respect for me, and since the doors opened of themselves, most certainly it is the time to-day for me to depart hence."

Then the groom accepted his lord's bidding, though he was aware of the purport of the king's orders, and, as if spurred on by another in his mind, he decided to bring the horse.

Then he brought for his master that noble steed, who was endowed with strength, mettle, speed and breeding. A golden bit filled his mouth and a light stall-blanket covered his back.

His chine and rump and fetlocks were long, while his hair, tail and ears were short and kept still; his back and flanks were depressed and raised, and the point of his nose, forehead, haunches and chest were broad.

The broadchested prince embraced him and patted him with a lotus-like hand, and ordered him in a gentle-toned voice, as if he were about to plunge into the middle of a hostile array.

"Oftentimes, I have been told, has the king, after mounting you, overthrown his enemies in battle. So act, O best of steeds, that I too may obtain the deathless stage.

Easy it is to find companions for battle, for the pleasure of acquiring the objects of sense and for the accumulation of wealth ; but hard it is for a man to find companions, when he has fallen into distress or attaches himself to *dharma*.

Moreover as for those who are companions in this world whether in action that brings defilement or in resort to *dharma*, undoubtedly they too, as my inner soul realises, take their share of the fruit.

Understand therefore, O best of steeds, this my departure from here to be connected with *dharma* for the benefit *of.* the world, and strive with speed and courage in a matter which concerns your own good and the good of the world alike."

Thus the best of men, beautiful in form and shining like black-tracked Agni, instructed the white horse, the best of steeds, in his duty as though he were a friend, and mounted him to go to the forest, just as the sun, blazing like fire, mounts a white autumnal cloud.

Thereon the good horse suppressed all noise, that would seem terrifying in the night-time or might awaken the attendants; his jaws were soundless and he silenced his neighing, as he went forth with steady steps.

Then the Yaksas bowed down their bodies and bore up his hoofs off the ground with the tips of their hands, that thrilled with joy; their forearms were adorned with golden bands and their hands were like lotuses, so that they seemed to be throwing lotuses beneath him.

The city gatehouses, which were closed with gates furnished with heavy bars and which could not easily have been forced even by elephants, opened noiselessly of their own accord as the king's son passed along.

Then he went forth out of his father's city, in the firmness of his resolve quitting without concern his father, who was devoted to him, his young son, his affectionate people and his unequalled magnificence.

Thereon he, whose eyes were long like stainless lotuses born of the mud, looked back at the city and uttered a lion roar–"I shall not be entering the city named after Kapila, till I have seen the further shore of life and death."

Hearing his words, the troops of the court of the Lord of Wealth rejoiced, and the hosts of gods with joyful minds foretold the fulfilment of his resolve.

Other heavenly beings of fiery forms recognised his purpose to be of the greatest difficulty and, like moon-beams piercing a rift in a cloud, produced a bright light on his frosty path.

But that steed, like a steed of the Sun, speeding on as if spurred in mind, and the prince travelled very many leagues, before the stars in the sky grew discoloured with the dawn.

6

THE DISMISSAL OF CHANDAKA

Then the world's eye, the sun, rose in a moment, and the best of men saw the hermitage of the descendant of Bhrgu.

When he saw it with the deer sleeping in perfect trust and the birds sitting at peace, he felt, as it were, rested and aa if the goal were attained.

In order to eschew arrogance and to show honour to asceticism, and in accordance with his politeness he dismounted from the horse.

And alighting, he patted his steed, saying, "Your task is accomplished", and well-pleased he said to Chandaka, bedewing him as it were with his eye:—

"In following this horse, whose speed is like that of Tarksya, you have shown, good friend, both loyalty to me and your own prowess.

Although I am entirely given up to other matters, I am gripped to the heart by you, who possess equally this devotion to your master in such a degree and also capability.

A man, though not devoted, may be capable, or though not capable, may be devoted; but it is hard to find in the world a man like you who is at the same time loyal and capable.

Therefore I am well-pleased with this your noble action in displaying towards me this feeling, which takes no count even of possible rewards.

Who would not be favourably disposed to a man in a position to reward him ? In the opposite case even kinsfolk for the most part become strangers.

The son is cherished to continue the family; the father is honoured to obtain maintenance. The attachment of the world is always due to some motive. No feeling that this or that person is one's kin subsists without a cause.

Why speak many words ? In short, you have done me a very great kindness. Return with the horse. I have arrived at the desired spot."

With these words the mighty prince unloosed his ornaments and gave them to Chandaka, whose mind smarted with sorrow, in order to do him a benefit.

Taking from his diadem the blazing jewel, which performed the function of a light, he stood like mount Mandara with the sun on it, and uttered these words:—

"With this jewel, Chanda, you must make repeated obeisance to the king, and in order to abate his grief you must in full confidence give him this message from me:—

"I have entered the penance grove to put an end to birth and death, and not forsooth out of yearning for Paradise, or out of lack of affection or out of anger.

Therefore you should not grieve for me, since I have left my home for this purpose. For a union, however long it has lasted, in time will cease to be.

And since separation is inevitable, therefore my thoughts turn to salvation, in order that there may be no more severing from my kindred.

You should not grieve for me, who have gone forth to leave grief behind. It is rather the slaves of passion, enthralled by those sources of grief, the loves, for whom grief should be felt.

And since this, they say, was the firm determination of our ancestors, grief should not be felt for me who am travelling along the hereditary road.

For when a man passes away, there are heirs to his wealth ; but heirs to *dharnna* are hard to find on earth or do not exist at all.

Should it be argued that this person has gone forth to the forest at the wrong time, I reply that there is no such thing as a wrong time for *dharma,* seeing how uncertain life is.

Therefore my determination is that the supreme good must be sought by me this very day. For when death is present as our adversary, what reliance can be placed on life ? "

In such wise, my good friend, should you speak to earth's guardian and also strive that he should not even think on me.

You should also tell the king that I am lacking in virtue. Lack of virtue causes the disappearance of affection; when affection has vanished, there is no sorrowing."

On hearing these words Chanda was overcome with anguish and, folding his hands, replied with a voice strangled with sobs:—

"At this disposition of yours, O my lord, which must cause distress to your kinsfolk, my mind sinks down like an elephant in the mud of a river.

To whom would not such a determination as this of yours cause tears, even if his heart were of iron, how much more when it is faltering with love ?

For this delicacy of limb, fitted only for lying in a palace, is not compatible with the ground of the penance grove, covered by sharp blades of *darbha-grass.*

But as for my bringing this horse to you after hearing your resolve, it was some divine power, O my lord, that forcibly caused me to do it.

For if I had been in command of myself, how could I, on knowing this your resolve, have brought you the horse, the bale of Kapilavastu ?

Therefore, O mighty prince, you should not desert, as a nihilist the good Law, your loving aged father, who yearns so for his son.

Nor should you forget, like an ingrate kind treatment, the queen, your second mother, who exhausted herself in bringing you up.

You should not abandon, like a coward the sovereignty he has obtained, the virtuous princess, mother of a young son, devotedly faithful to her husband and of illustrious lineage.

You should not abandon, like a vicious man his excellent repute, the young son of Yasodhara, worthy of praise and best of the cherishers of fame and *dharma.*

Or if, O my master, you are determined to abandon your father and your kingdom, you should not abandon me. For your feet are my sole refuge.

I cannot leave you in the forest, as Sumantra did Raghava, and go to the city with burning heart.

For what will the king say to me, if I return to the capital without you ? Or what shall I say to the women of your household, since I am in the habit of seeing what is proper.

As for your saying that I am also to tell the king of your lack of virtue, am I to say what is untrue about you, as about a sinless sage ?

Or if with halting tongue and shame in my heart I should so speak, who would believe it ?

For only the man who would tell of, or believe in, the scorching power of the moon, would tell of, or believe in, the existence of faults in you, who know the faults.

To desert the affectionate ill befits him who is always compassionate and ever feels pity. Turn back and have pity on me."

The best of speakers heard these words of the grief-stricken Chanda and spoke to him, self-possessed and with the utmost firmness:—

"Quit this affliction, Chanda, over parting from me; separation is the fixed law among corporeal beings, in that they are subject to different births.

Should affection lead me not to quit my kinsfolk of myself, still death would part us one from the other against our wills.

My mother bore me in her womb with pains and great longing. Her efforts have been fruitless. What am I to her now or she to me ?

As birds collect on the roosting tree and then go their separate ways again, so inevitably the union of beings ends in their parting.

And as the clouds come together and depart asunder again, so I deem the meeting and severance of creatures that draw breath.

And since this world is in a state of continuous separating, therefore the feeling that ' this is mine ' is improper with regard to a coming together that is transitory as a dream.

Trees are parted from the colouring of their leaves, though it is connate with them. How much more then must there be a severance of one thing from another that is separate from it ?

Since such is the case then, my good friend, be not afflicted; go your way. But if your affection tarries, still go and then return again.

And you should say to the folk in Kapilavastu, who keep regard for me, "Quit your love for him and hear his resolve.

Either, he says, he will quickly come back, after destroying-birth and death ; or, lacking in right effort and failing to reach the goal, he will perish."

On hearing his speech, Kanthaka, the finest of steeds, licked his feet and shed scalding tears.

With his webbed hand, which was marked with svastikas and bore the wheel sign on the palm, the prince stroked Kanthaka and spoke to him as if he were his comrade of like age—

"Do not shed tears, Kanthaka; you have displayed the qualities of a good horse. Be patient; this your toil will soon bring forth its fruit."

Then he resolutely took from Chanda's hand the sharp sword which had a jewelled hilt and was decorated with gold inlay, and drew it from the scabbard, as if he were drawing a snake from a hole.

Having unsheathed it with its blade dark blue as a blue lotus petal, he cut off his decorated headdress with the hair enclosed in it and tossed it with the muslin trailing from it into the air, as though tossing a goose into a lake.

And the inhabitants of Heaven caught it reverently, as it was thrown, with the intention of worshipping it, and the divine hosts paid it due adoration in Heaven with celestial honours.

But when he had divorced his ornaments and sheared

off the royal splendour of his head, he looked at his garments with their embroidery of golden geese, and in his steadfastness longed for a hermit's robe.

Then an inhabitant of Heaven of purified nature, knowing his thoughts, took on the form of a hunter of deer and approached him, wearing ochre-coloured clothes. To him the scion of the Sakya king spake:—

"Your holy ochre-coloured robe, the mark of a seer, does not go with this murderous bow. Therefore, good sir, if you are not attached to it, hand it over to me and accept this one of mine."

"O giver of desires", the hunter said, "although by this garment I cause the deer to trust me near them and then kill them, yet if, O Sakra-like prince, you have any use for it, take it then and give me the white one."

Then with the greatest joy he took the hermit's dress and gave up the silk raiment. But the hunter, assuming his heavenly form again, went to heaven with the white clothes.

Then, when he departed thus, the prince and the groom marvelled greatly and straight entertained all the more reverence for the forest dress.

Then he dismissed the weeping Chandaka and, wearing the ochre robe and bearing the fame of his steadfastness, moved majestically to where the hermitage was, resembling the monarch of the stars enveloped in a sunset cloud.

Then when his master went thence to the penance grove in his discoloured clothes and free from desire for rule, the groom flung up his arms and, wailing bitterly, fell to the ground.

Looking back once more, he wept aloud and clasped the hose, Kanthaka, with his arms. Then in despair he lamented again and again and started for the city with his body, but not with his mind.

Sometimes he brooded and sometimes he lamented, sometimes he stumbled and sometimes he fell. So journeying in grief under the force of his devotion, he performed many actions on the road in complete abandon.

7

PENANCE

Then since his state of longing for the forest had freed him from all attachments, Sarvarthasiddha left the weeping tear-faced Chanda and proceeded to the hermitage, overpowering it with his beauty, as if he were a Siddha.

With the gait of the king of beasts the prince entered that arena of deer, himself like a deer, and, though he had given up his royal trappings, the majesty of his person was such as to hold the eyes of the anchorites.

For the wheel-bearers, accompanied -by their wives and standing with their yoke-poles in their hands, gazed, just as they were, in their excitement on him who was like Indra, and did not stir, like beasts of burden with half-bowed heads.

And though the Brahmans, who had gone out to fetch fuel and had returned with their arms full of wood, flowers and *kusa* grass, were pre-eminent in austerities and had their minds fully trained, yet they went to see him and did not go to their huts.

And the peacocks rose up in delight and uttered cries as at the sight of a black rain-cloud; and the restless-eyed deer and the ascetics who grazed like deer let their grass fall and stood facing him.

And although the cows, that gave milk for the ablations, had already been milked, yet such was the joy produced in them at the sight of him, the lamp of the Iksvaku race, shining like the rising sun, that their teats flowed again.

"Is he the eighth Vasu or one of the Asvins come down to earth?" Such were the voices raised loud by the sages there in their amazement on seeing him.

For like a second form of the chief of the gods, or like the magnificence of the world of moving and stationary beings, he illumined the entire grove, as if he were the sun come down of his own accord.

Then, when those hermits duly honoured and invited him, he in return did honour to the supporters of *dharma* with a voice like a cloud full of rain.

Then he, who desired liberation, traversed the hermitage which was crowded with folk, desirous of Paradise and working to accumulate merit, and steadfastly he viewed their various austerities.

And when the benign one had viewed the various austerities of the ascetics in that penance grove, he thus addressed a certain anchorite who was following him, in order to ascertain the truth :—

"As I have never seen a hermitage till to-day, I am unacquainted with this method of *dharma*. Will you therefore kindly explain to me what is your resolve and to what point it is directed?"

Then the twice-born, who took delight in austerities, described in due order to the bull of the Sakyas, a very bull in prowess, the particularities of the austerities and the fruit thereof:—

"Uncultivated food, that which grows in the water, leaves, water, fruit and also roots, this is what the sages live on in accordance with the scriptures ; but there are various separate alternatives.

Some live like the birds by what they can pick up from the ground, others graze on grass like the deer, and others pass their time with the snakes, turned into anthills by the forest wind.

Some gain their subsistence by laborious pounding with stones, others eat only what has been husked by their own teeth, and some again cook for others and meet their needs on anything that may be left over.

Some with their coils of matted hair soaked with water twice offer oblations to Agni with sacred texts; others plunge into the water and dwell with the fishes, their bodies scored by turtles.

With such austerities accumulated for the due time, they win by the higher to Paradise, by the lower to the world of men. For bliss is obtained by the path of suffering; for bliss, they say, is the ultimate end of *dharma*."

The child of the lord of men listened to these and the like statements of the anchorites; though he liad not yet reached the perception of reality, he was not satisfied and said these words in an undertone to himself:—

"Seeing that asceticism in its varied kinds is suffering by nature, and that the reward of asceticism is Paradise at the highest, and that all the worlds are subject to change, truly this labour of the hermitages is to small effect.

Those who forsake their dear kindred and worldly pleasures to practise restraint for the sake of Paradise, truly they, when parted from its delights, will travel again to far greater bondage.

And he, who by the bodily toils known as austerities strives for the continuance of being in order to indulge passion, does not perceive the evils of the cycle of existence and seeks by suffering nothing but suffering.

Living creatures are ever in fear of death and yet they aim by their efforts at a fresh birth; and with the persistence of active being death is inevitable. Therefore they drown in that very thing of which they are afraid.

Some enter into labour for the sake of this world, others undergo toil for the sake of Paradise. Truly living beings, making themselves miserable in their hopes of bliss, miss their goal and fall into calamity.

It is not indeed that I blame the effort, which leaves aside the base and is directed to a higher object, but rather the wise with a like toil should do that in which the need for further effort ceases.

But if mortification of the body in this world is *dharma*, then the body's pleasure is contrary to *dharma;* if pleasure is obtained in the hereafter by means of *dharma*, then *dharma* in this world bears as its fruit what is contrary to *dharma*.

Inasmuch as it is under the direction of the mind that the body acts and ceases to act, therefore it is the taming of the mind only that is required. Apart from the mind the body is nothing but a log.

If merit is held to derive from purity of food, then merit accrues also to the deer and even to those men who are excluded from the rewards of *dharma* and on whom by some fault of their destiny wealth has turned its back.

But again, if it is the intention that is the cause of acquiring merit in the case of suffering, should not the same intention be applied in the case of pleasure ? Or if the intention is no criterion in the case of pleasure, is not the intention no criterion in the case of suffering ?

Similarly for those who sprinkle water on themselves to purify their deeds, acting on the assumption that it is a *tirtha,* in that case too their satisfaction is restricted to the feelings; for water will not make a sinner pure.

For if whatever water has been touched by the virtuous is claimed as a *tirtha on* earth, then it is only the virtues that I regard as the *tirtha,* but beyond all doubt the water is just water."

As he thus discussed various points with provision of many arguments, the sun went to its setting. Then he entered the grove, where was the holy quiet of austerities and where the trees were discoloured by the smoke of the oblations.

It was in full activity, a workshop as it were of *dharma,* with the transference elsewhere of the blazing sacrificial fires, with its throngs of seers who had completed their ablutions and with the shrines of the gods humming with the din of prayers.

And there he, who resembled the night-making orb, passed several nights, examining the austerities, and after considering them all and forming a judgement on them, he departed from that place of austerities.

Then the hermits followed him, their minds drawn to his beauty and majesty, just as great seers follow *Dharma,* as it withdraws from a land overrun by infidels.

Then he saw the ascetics with their fluttering coils of hair and clothes of bark, and in deference to their austerities he stopped by a beautiful auspicious tree on the roadside.

Thereon the hermits approached the best of men and stood round him, and the oldest of them addressed him respectfully with soft conciliatory words:—

"When you arrived, the hermitage became as it were full, with your departure it turns as it were into a desert. Therefore, my son, you should not quit us, as the loved life should not quit the body of one who wishes to live.

For in front stands the holy mountain Himavat, frequented by Brahman seers, royal seers and celestial seers; and by its neighbourhood these very austerities of the ascetics become multiplied in efficacy.

So too all round are holy pilgrimage places, very stairways to the sky and frequented by the celestial seers and the great seers who are self-controlled and whose beings are compact of *dharma.*

And from here again it is proper to pursue only the northern direction for the sake of the highest *dharma,* but it would not be fitting for the wise man to move even a single step towards the south.

But if you do not wish to live in the penance grove, because you have seen here one who neglects the rites or is impure from having fallen into an adulterated *dharma,* mention it and just be pleased to dwell here.

For we here desire to have you, who are as it were a depositary of asceticism, for our companion in asceticism. For to abide in company with you who are like Indra would bring success to Brhaspati."

When the chief of the ascetics had thus spoken in the midst of the ascetics, he, the chief of the wise, declared his inward feelings, inasmuch as he had made a vow for the annihilation of existence :—

"At such a display of their feelings towards me on the part of the upright-souled sages, the supporters of religion, whose delight in hospitality makes them like one's own kindred, my joy is extreme and I feel highly honoured.

To put it in a word, I am as it were bathed by these affectionate words, which touch my heart, and, as I am a novice in *dharma,* my pleasure now shows itself doubled.

When I reflect that I am about to go away, leaving you thus engaged, who are so hospitable and have shown me such very great kindness, I feel indeed as much grief as I did "when quitting my kinsfolk.

But your *dharma* aims at Paradise, while my desire is

for release from rebirth and leads me not to wish to dwell in this grove. For the *dharma* of cessation from activity is apart from the continuance of active being.

It is not for dissatisfaction on my part or for an offence committed by anyone else that I am going forth from this grove ; for you are all like the great seers, in that you take your stand on a *dharma* that conforms with the primeval ages."

Thus the prince spoke words, gracious and full of meaning, very gentle yet determined and dignified; and the ascetics then felt the highest degree of reverence for him.

But a certain twice-born there, who was in the habit of lying in the ashes, tall and with his hair in a tuft, clothed in tree-bark, with reddish eyes and a long thin nose, and carrying a waterpot in one hand, spoke to him thus :—

"Wise sir, noble in sooth is your resolve, in that, young as you are, you have seen the dangers of birth ; for he who, on a right consideration of Paradise and final salvation, decides for final salvation, only he truly exists in reality.

For those who are possessed by passion desire to go to Paradise by means of all those sacrifices, austerities and restrictions ; but those who have absolute goodness battle with passion as with an enemy and desire to attain liberation.

If therefore this is your settled purpose, go speedily to Vindhyakostha. There dwells the sage Arada, who has gained insight into final beatitude.

From him you will learn the path of the *tattvas,* and, if it pleases you, you will follow it. But since your resolution, I aee, is such, you will depart, rejecting his theory also.

For this face of yours has a straight high nose, large long eyes, a red lower lip with white sharp teeth, and a thin red tongue; and as such, it is sure to drink up to the very last drop the ocean of what is to be known.

But it is clear from your unfathomable depth, from your brilliance and from your bodily signs, that you will obtain on earth a position as teacher, such as was not won even by the seers of the golden age."

Then the king's son replied, " Very well", and, saluting the seers, proceeded on his way ; and the hermits too, after showing him due honour, entered the penance grove.

LAMENT

Then, when his master had gone to the forest in self-renouncement, the dejected groom did his utmost to repress his grief on the road; nevertheless his tears did not cease to flow.

But he now took eight days to traverse the same road, which by his lord's command he had covered in a single night with the horse; for he was ever thinking of the separation from his master.

And the horse Kanthaka, powerful as he was, travelled onward with flagging feelings and all his fire lost; and though decked with ornaments as before, yet without his master lie seemed to have lost his beauty.

And turning back towards the penance grove, he neighed loudly and often, in a mournful tone. And, though overcome with hunger, he took no pleasure on the road in grass or water as before and would not take either.

Then in due course they approached the city named after Kapila, which seemed empty like the sky without the sun, now that it was deserted by the magnanimous prince, whose being was concentrated on the weal of the world.

That very same city-grove, though still gay with lotus-covered waters and adorned with trees in full bloom, was now like a forest and no longer brilliant with citizens; for all their happiness had gone.

Then those two came slowly to the city as if going to a funeral bathing rite, while melancholy men wandered round them, depressed and with eyes struggling with tears, and seemed to stop them from proceeding.

And when the townsfolk saw the arrival of the pair without the bull of the Sakya race and that they were walking with drooping bodies, they shed tears in the road, as happened of old when the chariot of Dasaratha's son returned.

Thereon the folk burst into tears and followed behind Chandaka along the road, saying in the access of their grief, "Where is the king's son, the delight of the town and kingdom ? You have carried him off."

Then he said to those devoted people, " It is not I who am deserting the king's son. On the contrary, it was by him in the uninhabited forest that for all my tears I and the householder's garb were dismissed together."

When the people heard those words of his, they came to the conclusion that it was in truth a superhuman deed; for they did not restrain the tears that fell from their eyes and blamed the state of mind which arises from the fruit of the self.

Thereon again they said, "This very day let us go to the forest, where he, whose stride is as that of the king of elephants, has gone. Without him we have no wish to live, like embodied beings, when the senses have decayed.

This city without him is the forest, and that forest possessed of him the city. For without him our city has no beauty, like Heaven without the lord of the Maruts when Vrtra was slain."

Next the women betook themselves to the rows of windows, thinking that the prince had come back again, and when they perceived that the horse's back was empty, they shut the windows again and wailed aloud.

But the lord of men, who had undertaken religious observances for the recovery of his son and whose mind was afflicted by the vow and by grief, muttered prayers in the temples and performed various rites suitable to his intention.

Then the groom, leading the horse, entered the palace, with the tears welling from his eyes and overcome with grief as if his master had been carried off by an enemy warrior.

And Kanthaka, penetrating into the royal dwelling and looking round him with tear-streaming eye, cried out with a loud voice as if proclaiming his suffering to the people.

Then the birds which lived in the palace and the favourite horses which were tethered near by gave back the charger's cry, supposing the prince to have returned.

And the people who frequented the precincts of the queens' apartments were deceived by superabundant joy and thought from the way the horse Kanthaka neighed that the prince must be entering the palace.

The women rushed hopefully out of the buildings, like lightning flashing from an autumn cloud; they had been fainting with grief and now from the excess of their delight their eyes darted this way and that to see the prince.

Their hair was hanging down, their silk attire filthy, their faces without collyrium and their eyes struggling with tears; thus the women no more shone with their toilet unperformed than do the stars paling at night's close.

Their feet were without anklets and not stained red, their faces were without earrings and their necks unadorned, their hips, full by nature, were held in by no girdle, their breasts without their ropes of pearls looked as if they had been robbed.

The women's eyes flooded with tears, as they saw only Chandaka and the horse without their master; with downcast faces they wept, like cows lowing in the midst of the jungle when deserted by the herd-bull.

Then the lord of the earth's chief queen, Gautami, as affectionate for the son she had lost as a fond she-buffalo who has lost her calf, flung up her arms like a golden plantain-tree with leaves tossing about, and fell weeping to the ground.

Some of the other women, bereft of their brightness and with drooping arms and shoulders, seemed to become unconscious through despondency; they wailed not, they dropped no tears, they sighed not, they moved not, there they stood like figures in a picture.

Other women, losing self-control, swooned from grief for their lord, and with streams pouring down their faces their eyes watered their breasts from which the sandalwood was banished, as a mountain waters the rocks with its streams.

Then with the women's faces whipped by the water from their eyes the royal dwelling resembled a pond with dripping lotuses whipped by rain from the clouds at the time of the first rains.

As creepers waving in the wind strike themselves with their own tendrils, so these noble women beat their breasts with jewelless lotuslike hands, whose veins were hidden and whose fingers were plump and well-rounded so as to leave no interstices.

And thus, as their close-set upstanding breasts shook under the blows of their hands, those women looked like rivers with pairs of Brahminy ducks, which are made to tremble by the lotuses when blown about by the forest wind.

And as they hurt their breasts with their hands, so they hurt their hands with their breasts. There the women, all feelings of pity dulled, made their hands and breasts inflict mutual pains on each other.

But then up spoke Yasodhara, her eyes reddened with anger, her voice choking with the bitterness born of despair, her bosom heaving with sighs, and tears streaming down with the grief she was enduring :—

" Where, Chandaka, has he gone, my heart's desire, after deserting me at night against my will while I slept ? My mind trembles, when both you and Kanthaka have returned, while three went forth together.

Why do you weep here to-day, you brute, after doing me an ignoble, unkind, unfriendly deed ? Hold back your tears, be contented in mind. Tears go ill with that deed of yours.

For through you, his loving obedient faithful good companion, always doing what is proper, my lord has gone never to return. Rejoice, by good fortune your toil is rewarded with success.

Better is it for a man to have a wise enemy than a silly friend, who is skilful only in the wrong way. For your imprudence and so-called friendship have wrought great ruin for this family.

For these princesses with their ornaments laid aside and their eyes reddened and stained by incessant tears are sorely to be pitied like widows whose splendour has departed, though their lord is still in existence as much as are the Himalayas or the earth.

And these rows of pavilions seem to weep together with the women, on separation from him, casting up their pinnacles for arms and heaving long sighs with their enamoured doves.

This horse Kanthaka too must have been desirous of my ruin in every way; for, when everyone was asleep at night, he thus carried off my treasure from here, like a jewel-thief.

Seeing that he is certainly able to stand up even to the strokes of the arrows that fall on him, not to speak of the whip, how was it he went off under fear of the fall of the whip, taking with him my good fortune and my heart together ?

To-day the base creature neighs loudly, filling as it were the royal abode; but when he was carrying away my beloved, it was then that the wretched horse was dumb.

For if he had neighed and so woken up the people, or if he had made a noise with his hoofs, or if he had made the loudest sound he could with his jaws, such suffering would not have come on me."

When Chandaka heard the princess's words, with their undercurrent of lament and with their syllables strangled with sobs, he looked downwards and, folding his hands, he muttered this answer in a low voice, hardly intelligible through his tears.

"Princess, you should not disparage Kanthaka nor should you be angry with me. Know us to be entirely guiltless. For the god among men. Princess, departed like a god.

For, although I knew the king's command, I was compelled as it were by certain divine beings and speedily brought him this horse. Thus too I felt no weariness in following him along the road.

This best of steeds too, as he went along the road, did not touch the ground with the tips of his hoofs, as if he were held up off from it in the air ; similarly his mouth was restrained as if through divine power, so that he did not make any noise with his jaws or neigh.

Seeing that, when the king's son went forth, the gate was thrown open at that time of itself and the darkness of night was broken through by what seemed to be the sun, this therefore too must be understood to have been of divine ordering.

Seeing that the people by thousands in the palace and city, observant though they were of the king's command, did not awake at that time but were overcome by sleep, this therefore too must be understood to have been of divine ordering.

And seeing that a garment, suitable for forest wear, was handed over to him at the time by a denizen of Heaven, and that his headdress was borne off, when thrown into the sky, this therefore too must be understood to have been of divine ordering.

Therefore with regard to his departure you should not, Princess, consider us two to be at fault. Neither I nor the horse acted of our own will; for he went forth with the gods in attendance."

When those women heard thus of his wondrous departure with its accompaniment of many gods, they were lost in amazement as if their grief had gone, but they became the prey of mental fever because of his taking up the mendicant's life.

Then Gautami, with eyes restless with despair, lost her self-control and wailed aloud in her suffering, like an osprey that has lost its nestlings ; she swooned and with tearstrewn face exclaimed :—

"Have those hairs of his which are worthy of being encircled, by a royal diadem, been cast to the ground, hairs which were soft, black and glossy, in great locks and curling upwards with each hair growing separately from its own orifice ?

His arms are long, his gait that of the king of beasts, his eyes like a mighty bull's, his chest broad, his voice like the drum of the gods, and he shines with the brilliance of gold. Ought such a one to live in a hermitage ?

Is this earth then not to have its portion of that peerless, noble-doing lord ? He has gone from here ; for it is only through the good fortune and virtues of the subjects that such a virtuous ruler of men is born.

His feet are soft with a beautiful network spread over the toes, tender as the fibre of a lotus or a flower, with the anklebones concealed and wheels in the middle of the soles. Shall they tread on the hard ground of the jungle ?

His powerful body is accustomed to sitting or lying on the palace roof and has been adorned with priceless clothes, aloes and sandalwood. How will it fare in the forest in the heat, the cold and the rains ?

He is ennobled by race, goodness, strength, beauty, learning, majesty and youth, and so fitted to give, not to ask. Is he to practise begging alms from others ?

He has been sleeping on a spotless golden bed and awakened at night by the strains of musical instruments. How then shall he lie in accordance with his vows on the ground with only a piece of cloth interposed ? "

Hearing these piteous ravings, the women clasped one another with their arms and let fall tears from their eyes, as shaken creepers drop honey from their flowers.

Then Yasodhara fell upon the ground, like a Brahminy duck without its mate, and in her distress she uttered all sorts of laments with a voice that was repeatedly held back by sobs:—

'If he wishes to carry out *dharma* and yet casts me off, his lawful partner in the duties of religion and now husbandless, in what respect is there *dharma* for him who wishes to follow austerities separated from his lawful partner ?

Surely he has not heard of our ancestors, Mahasudarsa and the other kings of old, who took their wives with them to the forest, since he thus intends to carry out *dharma* without me.

Or else he does not see that in the sacrifices it is both husband and wife who are consecrated and purified by the precepts of the Veda and who will enjoy together in the hereafter too the recompense of the rites ; therefore he has become miserly of *dharma* towards me.

Being distinguished for *dharma,* he must have held my mind to be secretly and repeatedly given to jealousy and quarrelling; so lightly and without fear deserting me as being of a wrathful nature, he wishes to obtain the Apsarases in great Indra's heaven.

But I am anxious on this point, namely, what kind of excellent beauty is possessed by the women in that world, for whose sake he gave up sovereign glory and my devotion too and is practising austerities.

It is not in truth that I envy him the delights of Paradise; their acquisition is not difficult even for an ordinary person like me. But my one desire is to secure that my beloved shall not leave me either in this life or in the hereafter.

If it is not to be my lot to look up at the sweetly-smiling long-eyed face of my lord, still is this poor Rahula never to be dandled in his father's lap ?

Alas ! If my lord is tender in body and high in spirit, how cruel and exceeding hard is his mind, when in sooth he abandons such an infant son with his babbling talk, who would charm even an enemy.

My heart too is certainly exceeding hard, made of stone or even of iron, in that it does not break in its orphaned state, when my lord, accustomed to all pleasures, has departed to the forest without his royal glory."

In such terms the princess, fainting with grief for her husband, wept and brooded and lamented repeatedly. For, though steadfast by nature, she forgot the rules of decorum and felt no shame.

When the women saw Yasodhara lying there on the ground, undone by grief and lamentation, they mourned aloud and their faces with the tears on them looked like mighty lotuses whipped by the rain.

But, his prayers ended and the auspicious oblations completed, the king came out of the temple and, smitten by the distressed wail of the people, trembled like an elephant at the roar of a thunderbolt.

And perceiving the two of them, Chandaka and Kanthaka, and hearing of his son's firm resolve, the lord of the earth was overwhelmed with grief and fell down like the banner of Saci's lord when the festival is over.

Then for a moment he swooned with grief for his son and was held up by persons of birth equal to his own ; and still on the ground he fixed the horse with tearful gaze and thus lamented :—

"Many, Kanthaka, are the services you have rendered me in battle; one great disservice you have done me in that, though you do love him, you have thrown off in the jungle my loved one, who is so fond of virtue, as if you did not love him.

Therefore either take me at once there where he is, or go quickly and bring him back again. For without him no more is there life for me than for a man fallen ill who lacks the right medicine.

Samjaya achieved the impossible by not dying when Suvarnanisthivin was carried off by death; I however, now that my *dharma*-loving son has departed wish to yield up my soul like one who has no self-control.

For would not the mind even of Manu have been distracted, if parted from a dear virtuous son, Manu, the son of Vivasvat, the knower of the former and the latter things, the mighty lord of creation, from whom issued ten races of kings ?

I envy the king, the friend of Indra, the wise son of king Aja, who when his son departed to the forest, went to Heaven instead of continuing to live in misery with futile tears.

Point out to me, good steed, that hermitage-place to which you carried off him who is to give me the funeral water. For these my vital airs are about to travel the way of the departed and long for him in the desire to drink the draught."

Thus the king grieved over the separation from his son and lost his steedfastness, though it was innate like the solidity of the earth; and as if in delirium, he uttered many laments, like Dasaratha dominated by grief for Rama.

Then the counsellor, who was endowed with learning, decorum and virtue, and the aged purohita addressed him thus as was proper in a well-balanced manner, neither distressed in face nor yet untouched by sorrow :—

"Cease grieving, O best of men, return to firmness; you should not, O steadfast one, shed tears like a man without Itself-control. For many kings on earth have cast aside their sovereignty like a crushed wreath and entered the forests.

Moreover this his state of mind was predestined; call to mind the words of the seer Asita of old. For it is not possible to make him stay happily even for a moment in Paradise or in a Cakravartin's rulership.

But if, O best of men, the effort can be carried out at all, quickly give the word and we will go there at once. Just let there be a struggle of many kinds on this point between your son and the various prescriptions of scripture."

Thereon the king ordered them, " Therefore do you two set out speedily from this very spot. For my heart, like that of a forest bird hankering after its young, finds no peace."

"Very well ", said the minister and purohita and at the king's command they left for the forest. The king too, considering the matter to have been successfully disposed of, performed the remaining rites in company with his wives and daughters-in-law.

9

THE DEPUTATION TO THE PRINCE

Then at that time the counsellor and the purohita, spurred on by the king with the goad of words, set out for the forest with the speed of devotion and made every effort like noble steeds when pricked.

In due course and accompanied by a suitable retinue, they reached the hermitage, wearied out by their exertions. Discarding their official pomp and assuming a sober demeanour, they proceeded straight to the abode of the descendant of Bhrgu.

They did reverence to the Brahman in accordance with propriety and were duly honoured by him. When they had been given seats and the Bhargava had taken his, they entered on their tale and stated their business :—

"Know us two to be charged with the preservation of the sacred traditions and with the practice of counsel respectively for the royal scion of Iksvaku's line, who is pure in his might, pure in his widespreading fame.

He who resembles Indra has a son resembling Jayanta, who, we hear, has come to this place in his desire to pass beyond the dangers of old age and death. Your Holiness should know that we have come on his account."

He answered them, " The long-armed prince did come here, a boy in years but of fully developed intelligence. But, understanding that our rule of life leads to rebirth, he went on to seek Arada in his desire for salvation."

Then on learning the true state of affairs from him, they immediately bade farewell to the sage, and started off in the direction the prince had taken, wearied indeed but in their devotion to the king as if unwearied.

Then as they went along, they saw him sitting on the road at the foot of a tree, not adorned with the artifices of the toilet but blazing with his form, like the sun when it has entered a circle of cloud.

Then leaving the chariot, the purohita, accompanied by the counsellor, went up to him, as the seer, the son of Urvasi, accompanied by Vamadeva, approached Rama when he was in the forest.

They paid him due honour, as Sukra and the son of Angiras did to the mighty Indra in heaven, and he paid them due honour in return, as the mighty Indra did to Sukra and the son of Angiras in heaven.

Then obtaining his permission, they sat down on either side of the banner of the Sakya race and, thus close to him, they resembled the twin stars of Punarvasu in conjunction with the moon.

The purohita addressed the king's son as he sat, shining gloriously, at the foot of the tree, just as Brhaspati addressed Indra's son Jayanta, as he sat in Paradise by the *parijata* tree :—

" Listen, Prince, to this that the king said to you, with his eyes raining tears, when he was stupefied for a moment on the ground with the dart of grief for you plunged into his heart :—

"I know of your fixed resolve with regard to *dharma* and I realise that this will be your future goal. But by reason of your proceeding to the forest at the wrong time I am burnt up with the fire of grief as with a real fire.

Therefore come, lover of *dharma,* to do me a favour, and give up this purpose for the very sake of *dharma.* For the current of my grief has swollen and is afflicting me, as the swollen current of a river cuts away the bank.

For the actions, which the wind, the sun, fire and the thunderbolt exercise on a cloud, water, dry grass and a mountain respectively, are being exercised on me by grief with its dispersing, drying up, burning and shattering.

Therefore enjoy lordship for the present over the earth and you shall go to the forest at the time approved by the Scriptures. Have regard for me, your unlucky father ; for *dharma* consists in compassion for all creatures.

Nor is it only in the forest that this *dharma* is achieved; its achievement is certain for the self-controlled in a city too. Purpose and effort are the means in this matter ; for the forest and the badges of mendicancy are the mark of the faint-hearted.

The *dharma* of salvation has been attained by kings, even though they remained at home, wearing the royal tiara, with strings of pearls hanging over their shoulders and their arms fortified by rings, as they lay cradled in the lap of imperial; Fortune.

The two younger brothers of Dhruva, Bali and Vajra-bahu, Vaibhraja, Asadha and Antideva, Janaka the Videha king, .. . Druma and the Senajit kings,

All these lords of men, you must know, were versed in the method of practising the *dharma* that leads to final beatitude, while still remaining in their homes. Therefore resort even to both at onee, lordship over knowledge and royal sovereignty.

For it is my wish to embrace you closely while you are still wet with the coronations waters, to behold you beneath the imperial umbrella, and with the selfsame joy to proceed to the forest."

So spoke the king to you with a speech whose utterance was strangled by tears. You should listen and, to do him pleasure, you should follow after his love with love.

The Sakya king is drowning in the unplumbed ocean of suffering, which originates from you and whose waters are grief. Therefore rescue him who is without a protector or support, as a ship rescues a man drowning without support in the ocean.

Hearing of the deeds done by Bhisma, who sprang from the womb of Ganga, Rama, and Rama the descendant of Bhrgu, to please their fathers, you also should do what your father wants.

Know that the queen, who brought you up, weeps piteously and incessantly in distress like a fond cow who has lost her calf, and has almost gone to the region over which Agastya presides.

You should save by the sight of yourself your wretched wife, who, though not a widow, is husbandless and resembles a goose separated from her mate or a cow-elephant abandoned in the forest by the bull-elephant.

Deliver Rahula from grief for his parent as the full moon from eclipse by Rahu; he is your only gon, an infant unfitted for suffering, yet bearing the smart of sorrow in his heart.

The palace and the entire city are being burnt up with the fire of grief, whose fuel is separation from you, whose smoke is aighs and whose flames sorrow, and they long for the water of a sight of you."

The Bodhisattva, fulfilled in resolution, listened to the words of the purohita, and after a moment's meditation, in his knowledge of all qualities, he thus made, an excellent and courteous reply:—

"I am fully aware of the feelings fathers have for their sons, more especially that which the king has for me ; but though know it, I am afraid of disease, old age and death and have no alternative but to quit my kindred.

For, if in the end there were not parting from one's dear ones, who would not wish to see his dear kinsfolk ? But since, however long delayed, separation does take place, I quit even my affectionate father.

As for your mention of the king's grief on my behalf, it does not please me that he should feel distress, since unions are fleeting as dreams and parting is certain.

And, perceiving the mutable course of the world, your mind should come thus to this conclusion that the cause oi affliction is neither the son nor the father; this distress is the outcome of ignorance.

The separation of creatures who have come together in this world, as of wayfarers, ia inevitable in the course of time. What wise man then would cherish grief, when forsaken by those who are only his kindred in name ?

A man comes hither, abandoning his kindred in the previous existence; and he gives them the slip in this life and journeys on again ; after going to the next existence too, he goes to a further one. How can there be attachment to folk who are ever deserting others ?

And since from the womb onwards in all circumstances Death is ready to strike, why does His Majesty in his love for his son describe my departure to the forest as being at the wrong time ?

There is a wrong time for giving oneself up to the objects of the senses; similarly a time is prescribed for the means to wealth. At all seasons Time constrains the world; Time does not exist in the highest good which leads to salvation.

And as for the king's desire to hand the kingdom over to me, that too is noble and worthy of a father, but it would not be right for me to accept it, like a sick man greedily accepting unwholesome food.

In what way could it be right for a wise man to take sovereignty on himself ? It is the abode of delusion in which are to be found tearfulness, the intoxication of pride, weariness and loss of *dharma* by the mishandling of others,

For kingship is at the same time full of delights and the vehicle of calamity, like a golden palace all on fire, like dainty food mixed with poison, or like a lotus-pond infested with crocodiles.

And thus kingship is neither pleasure nor *dharma, so* that the kings of old, when age came on with its unavoidable suffering, felt disgust and, giving up their kingdoms, betook themselves to the forest.

For it is better to eat herbs in the forest, embracing the highest contentment as if one were concealing a jewel, than to live with the dangers to which sovereignty is exposed, as if with loathsome black snakes.

For it is praiseworthy for kings to leave their kingdoms and enter the forest in the desire for *dharma,* but it is not fitting to break one's vow and forsaking the forest to go to one's home.

For what man of resolution and good family, having once gone to the forest in the desire for *dharma*, would cast off the robe and, dead to shame, proceed to the city even of Puramdara ?

For only the man, who from greed, delusion or fear, would take again the food he has vomited up, would from greed, delusion or fear, abandon the lusts of the flesh and then return to them.

And the man, who, after escaping with difficulty from a burning house, would enter that very house again, only he, after giving up the state of a householder, because he aees its dangers, would desire out of delusion to assume it again.

As for the tradition that kings obtained fines emancipation while remaining in their homes, this is not the case : How can the of salvation in which quietude predominates reconciled with the *dharma* of kings in which seuerity of action predominates?

If a king delights in quietude, his kingdom collapses; if his mind turns to his kingdom, his quietude is rained. For quietude and severity are incompatible, like the union of water which is cold with fire which is hot.

Either therefore those lords of the earth resolectly cast aside their kingdoms and obtained quietuder or stained by kingship, they claimed to have attained lineration on the ground that their senses were under control, but infact only reached a state that was not final.

Or let it be conceded they duly attained quietude while holding kingship, still I have not gone to the forest with an undecided mind; for having cut through the net known s home and kindred I am freed and have no intention of re-entering the net."

Thus spoke the king's son with vigour, freed from all ambition in accordance with his virtues and self-knowledge, and adducing good arguments. The counsellor too, hearing him, thus made reply:—

It is not that your resolution for the practice of *dharma* is unfitting in itself, but only that the present is not the time for it. For it could not be your *dharma,* delighting in *dharma* as you do, to deliver up your father in his old age to grief.

And surely your intellect is not subtle or else is short-sighted in the matter of *dharma,* wealth and pleasure, that you should despise the object before your eyes in favour of an unseen result and so depart.

And some say there is rebirth, others confidently assert that there is not. Since this matter is thus in doubt, it is proper to enjoy the sovereignty that offers itself to you.

If there is any continuance of activity hereafter, we shall enjoy ourselves in it according to the birth we obtain ; but if there is no continuance of activity in another existence, this world accomplishes liberation without any effort on its part.

Some say there is a future life but do not explain the means of liberation. They teach that there is an essential force of nature at work in the continuance of activity, like the essential heat of fire and the essential liquidity of water.

Some explain that good and evil and existence and non-existence originate by natural development; and since all this world originates by natural development, again therefore effort is vain.

That the action of each sense is limited to its own class of object, that the qualities of being agreeable or disagreeable is to be found in the objects of the senses, and that we are affected by old age and afflictions, in all that what room is there for effort ? Is it not purely a natural development ?

The oblation-devouring fire is stilled by water, and the flames cause water to dry up. The elements, separate by nature, group themselves together into bodies and, coalescing, constitute the world.

That, when the individual enters the womb, he develops hands, feet, belly, back and head, and that his soul unites with that body, all this the doctors of this school attribute to natural development.

Who fashions the sharpness of the thorn or the varied nature of beast and bird ? All this takes place by natural development. There is no such thing in this respect as action of our own will, *a fortiori* no possibility of effort.

So others say that creation proceeds from Isvara. What is the need in that case for action by man ? The very same being, who *is* the cause in the continuing activity of the world, is certainly also the cause in its ceasing to be active.

There are others who assert that the coming into being and the passing away from being is solely on account of the soul. But they explain coming into being as taking place without effort, and declare the attainment of liberation to be by effort.

On the ground that a man discharges his debt to his ancestors by the procreation of offspring, to the seers by the Vedas, to the gods by sacrifices, that he is born with these three debts on him, and that whoever obtains release from them obtains that which alone can be called liberation.

The doctors declare that liberation is for him only who strives thus in accordance with these Vedic injunctions; for those, who desire liberation by means of their individual energy, however much they exert themselves, reap nothing but weariness.

So, my good air, if you are attached to liberation, follow in due form the injunctions I have just described. Thus you will obtain liberation and the king's grief will be brought to an end.

As for your idea that it is wrong to go back to the palace from the penance groves, be not disturbed, my son, on that score either; those of old went to their own families from the forests.

Although he was living in the penance grove surrounded by his subjects, Ambarisa went back to his city; so too Rama left the penance grove and protected the earth, when it was oppressed by the infidel.

Similarly the king of the Salvas called Druma with his son entered the city from the forest, and Antideva, the Samkrti, who was a Brahman seer, accepted the royal dignity from the sage, Vasistha.

Such as these, who blazed with the fame of *dharma,* gave up the forest and proceeded to their palaces. Therefore there is nothing wrong in going home from the penance grove, when it is for the sake of *dharma.*"

The prince listened to the affectionate words, meant for his good, of the counsellor, the king's eye, and then taking his stand on steadfastness, gave him a reply, which met every point without being over-discursive and was devoid of attachment as well as measured in tone :—

"As for this disputed question of existence and non-existence in this universe, no decision is possible for me on the strength of another's words. I will arrive at the truth for myself by asceticism and quietude and will accept what is determined accordingly in this matter.

For it would not be proper for me to accept a doctrinal system, which is born of doubt and is obscure and mutually contradictory. For what wise man would go forward in dependence on another, like a blind man with a blind leader in the dark ?

But although I have not yet seen the final truth, still if the reality of good and evil is in dispute, my decision is for the good. For better is the toil, though vainly, of the man who devotes himself to the good than the bliss, even though in the real truth, of the man who gives himself up to what is contemptible.

But seeing that the scriptural tradition is uncertain, understand that to be good which is spoken by the authorities, and understand that the only basis for authority is the expulsion of sin. For he who has expelled sin will not speak what is false.

And as for your quoting the instances of Rama and the others to justify my return, they do not prove your case; for those who have broken their vows are not competent authorities in deciding matters of *dharma.*

Such being the case, the sun may fall to the earth, Mount Himavat may lose its firmness, but I will not return to my family as a worldly man who has not seen the final truth and whose senses are drawn towards the objects of pleasure.

I would enter a blazing fire, but I would not enter my home with my goal unattained," Thus he proudly made his asseveration and, rising in accordance with his declaration, he departed in all selflessness.

Then the minister and the Brahman, perceiving his resolution to be unshakable, tearfully followed him, grieving and with faces downcast, then slowly for lack of other resource wended their way to the city.

Then out of affection for him and devotion to the king, they turned back full of cares and stood still; for, as he blazed with his own brightness, as unapproachable as the sun, they could neither look on him on the road nor yet quit him.

And they deputed trustworthy spies in disguise in order to know the way taken by him whose way was the highest, and with much difficulty they set off, thinking how they were to go and see the king who was thirsting for his dear son.

10

SRENYA'S VISIT

So the prince of the broad stout chest dismissed the officers who were in charge of the king's sacrifices and his council chamber, and passing over the tossing waves of the Ganges, he came to Rajagrha of the lordly palaces.

As peacefully as Svayambhu proceeding to the highest heaven, he entered the city distinguished by its five hills, which is guarded and adorned by mountains and supported and purified by auspicious hot springs.

The people there at that time, perceiving his gravity and might and his glorious form surpassing that of mankind, as of him who has taken the pillar vow and has the bull for his sign, were lost in amazement.

On seeing him, whoever was going in another direction stood still; whoever was standing in the road followed him; whoever was going quickly went slowly, and whoever was sitting down sprang up.

Some worshipped him with joined hands, others honoured him by saluting him with their heads, others greeted him with kindly words ; none passed on without doing him reverence.

On seeing him, the gaudily-dressed felt ashamed and the chatterers on the roadside fell silent; as in the presence of Dharma incarnate none think thoughts not directed to the way of salvation, so no one indulged in improper thoughts.

The gaze of the women or men on the royal highroad, busied though they were with other affairs, was not satiated with looking most reverently on the godlike son of the human god.

His brows, his forehead, his mouth or his eyes, his form or his hands, his feet or his gait, whatever part of him anyone looked at, to that part his eyes were riveted.

And Rajagrha's Goddess of Fortune was perturbed on seeing him, who was worthy of ruling the earth and was yet in a bhiksu's robe, with the circle of hair between his brows, with the long eyes, radiant body and hands beautifully webbed.

Then Srenya, lord of the Magadha land, saw from an outer pavilion the mighty concourse of people and enquired the reason thereof. Then an officer explained it to him:—

"This is the son of the Sakya monarch, of whom the Brahmans said he would attain either supreme knowledge or lordship over the whole earth. He has become a wandering mendicant and the people are gazing at him."

Then the king, on hearing the reason, was excited in mind and said to the same officer," "Find out where he is stopping ". " Very well ", he replied and followed the prince.

But with moveless eyes looking only a yoke's length ahead, voice stilled and walk slow and restrained, he, the best of mendicants, kept his limbs and active mind under control and begged his food.

And accepting the alms without distinction, he proceeded to a lonely rivulet of the mountain, and after taking his meal there in due form he climbed Mount Pandava.

On that mountain, fledged with groves of *lodhra* trees and with its glades resounding with peacocks' calls, he, the sun of mankind, appeared in his ochre-coloured robe like the sun in the early morning above the eastern mountain.

The royal officer, seeing him there, informed king Srenya, and the king, on hearing the news, set off, but only with a modest retinue from his feeling of veneration.

In heroism the peer of Pandu's son, in stature like a mountain, he ascended Pandava the best of mountains; this lion-man, with the gait of a lion and wearing a royal tiara, resembled a lion with shaking mane.

Then he saw the Bodhisattva, sitting cross-legged with tranquil senses, being as it were a peak of the mountain and shining like the moon rising out of a bower of clouds.

As he sat there in the majesty of his beauty and in holy tranquillity, like some being magically projected by Dharma, the lord of men drew near him with amazement and deference, as Sakra drew near Svayambhu.

And as he came in fitting manner up to him, who was the best of those who know the Plan, he enquired about his health, and he too with equal courtesy spoke to the king about his peace of mind and freedom from illness.

Then the king sat down on a clean piece of rock, dark blue as an elephant's ear, and being seated beside him with his permission spoke to him, desiring to ascertain his state of mind :—

"I have a strong friendship for your family, which has come down by inheritance and has been well tested ; hence, my friend, my desire to speak with you. So listen to these words of affection.

Your family is mighty, originating from the Sun, your age the prime of youth, this your beauty radiant. Why then this decision of yours, out of all due order, to delight in alms-seeking instead of in kingship ?

For your limbs are worthy of red sandalwood, not meant for contact with the ochre robe. That hand is fitted for protecting subjects and does not deserve to take food given by another.

Therefore, my friend, if out of love for your father you do not wish for your hereditary kingdom by force and if you do not care to wait for the succession in due course, accept straightway the half of my realm.

For thus there will be no need to oppress your kinsfolk, and in course of time sovereignty will come to you peacefully. Therefore do me this kindness ; for association with the good makes for the prosperity of the good.

Or if now from pride of race you cannot show your trust in me, with me as your comrade plunge into the arrayed battle-lines with arrows and conquer your foes.

Choose therefore one or other of these alternatives, and in all propriety devote yourself to *dharma,* wealth and pleasure ; for by confusing these three objects in this world out of passion, men go to ruin in the next world as well as in this.

For if the entire goal is desired, you must give up that pleasure which is obtained by suppressing *dharma* and wealth, and that wealth which is obtained by overpowering *dharma* and pleasure, and that *dharma* which is obtained by the cessation of wealth and pleasure.

Therefore by pursuit of the triple end of life make this beauty of yours bear fruit; for they say that the complete attainment of *dharma,* wealth and pleasure is for mankind the complete object of the individual.

Therefore you should not let these two stout arms, fitted for drawing the bow, lie useless; for like Mandhatr's, they are capable of conquering even the three worlds, how much more this earth here ?

Truly I say this to you out of affection, not out of love of dominion or arrogance ; for, seeing this bhiksu's robe of yours, I am moved to compassion and tears come to my eyes.

Therefore, lover of the mendicant's stage of life, enjoy the pleasures, before old age comes again on you, the pattern of your race, and confounds your beauty ; in due time, lover of *dharma,* you will perform *dharma.*

The aged truly can obtain *dharma* and age has no capacity for enjoying the pleasures. And therefore they attribute the pleasures to youth, wealth to middle age, *dharma* to the old.

For, in the world of the living, youth is naturally opposed to *dharma* and wealth, and, however tightly checked, it is hard to hold, so that the pleasures carry it off by that path.

Old age is given to reflection, grave and intent on stability; with little labour it acquires holy tranquillity, partly from incapacity for anything else, partly from shame.

Therefore when men have passed through the restless, deceptive period of youth, which is given up to the objects of the senses, heedless, intolerant, and short-sighted, they breathe again as if they had safely crossed a desert.

Therefore just let this unbalanced time of youth pass away with its heedlessness and rebelliousness ; for the flush of youth is a target for the God of Love and cannot be protected from the senses.

Or if *dharma* is really your intention, offer sacrifices; that is the *dharma* of your family. For taking possession of the highest heaven by means of sacrifices, Marutvat also went to the highest heaven.

For with their arms marked by rings of gold and their headdresses bright with the glitter of radiant jewels, the royal seers travelled through sacrifices the very same path that the great seers reached by their austerities."

Such was the speech of the king of Magadha, who in speaking rightly resembled Valabhid. The king's son heard it, but wavered no more than the mountain of Kailasa shakes with its many sparkling peaks.

11

PASSIONS SPURRED

Thereon, when the Magadha king spoke to him with friendly face but with matter that was repugnant to him, the son of Suddhodana, who was purified by the spotlessness of his race, remained calm and unmoved and addressed this reply to him:—

"There is nothing for wonderment..., that you should behave thus towards your friends, when you spring from the illustrious family of Haryanka and from the purity of your conduct are so devoted to your friends.

Like sovereignty among cowards, friendship, inherited in their families, does not stand firm among the vicious; but the virtuous increase the same friendship, originated by their ancestors, with an uninterrupted succession of friendly acts.

And those men in the world I hold to be truly friends, who share in the enterprises of their friends when in straits. For who in this world would not be a friend to a man who is at ease in the enjoyment of prosperity ?

And thus those who, gaining riches in the world, employ them on behalf of their friends or of *dharma,* obtain the full value of their wealth, and, if it is lost, it causes them no pain at the end.

Certainly this resolution of yours regarding me, O king, proceeds from friendship and nobility of heart. I shall content you about it with similar friendship; I would not answer you in any other wise in this matter.

Because I recognise the danger of old age and death, I have betaken myself to this *dharma* out of longing for salvation and have quitted my tearstained relations, and still more therefore the passions, the causes of evil.

For I am not so afraid of venomous snakes or of thunderbolts that fall from the sky or of fire allied with the wind, as I fear the objects of the senses.

For the passions are ephemeral, robbers of the treasury of good, empty, like will-o'-the-wisps in the world. The mere expectation of them deludes men's minds, how much more then their actual possession ?

For the victims of the passions find no relief in the triple heaven, still less in the world of mortals. For the lustful man can no more win satiety from the passions, than a fire companioned by the wind can from fuel.

There is no calamity in the world equal to the passions, and it is to them that mankind in their delusions are attached. What wise man, afraid of calamity and recognising the truth to be thus, would of himself yearn for calamity ?

Even when they have won the earth, girdled by the sea, they wish to extend their conquests beyond the great ocean. There is no satiety for man with the passions, as for the ocean with the waters that fall into it.

Though the heavens rained gold for him and though he conquered the whole of the four continents and won half the seat of Sakra, yet Mandhatr's longing for the objects of sense remained unappeased.

Although he enjoyed sovereignty over the gods in heaven, when Satakratu hid himself for fear of Vrtra, and though out of wanton pride he made the great rsis carry him, yet Nahusa fell, being still unsatisfied with the passions.

Although the royal son of Ida penetrated the triple heaven and brought the goddess Urvasi into his power, he was still unsatisfied with the objects of sense and came to destruction in his greedy desire to seize gold from the rsis.

Who would trust in those objects of sense, which are subject to disturbance by all sorts of fate, either in heaven or on earth, seeing that they passed from Bali to great Indra, from great Indra to Nahusa and from Nahusa back again to great Indra?

Who would seek after the enemies known as the passions, by whom even sages were undone, despite their bark-dresses, their diet of roots and water, their coils of hair long as snakes, and their lack of worldly interests.

For their sake Ugrayudha, armed though he was with a terrible weapon, met death at the hands of Bhisma. The mere thought of them is unlucky and fatal to the well-conducted, still more so therefore to those not restrained by vows.

Who would swallow the poison known as the passions, when he knows how paltry is the flavour of the objects of sense, how great the bondage, how incomplete the satisfaction, how much despised by the good, and how certain the sin ?

It is right for the self-controlled to cast aside the passions, when they hear of the suffering of the passion-ridden, afflicted as they are by pursuits such as agriculture, etc., and of the well-being of those whom the passions fail to excite.

Success in the passions is to be recognised as a misfortune for the passionate man; for he becomes intoxicated by achievement of the passions, and because of intoxication he does what he should not, not what he should, and wounded thereby, he obtains rebirth in a lower sphere.

What wise man in this world would delight in those passions, which are only won and retained by labour and which cheating men, depart again, as though they were loans borrowed for a time ?

What self-controlled man in the world would deliglit in those passions, which are like a torch of grass ? When men seek and hold them, they excite desire, and if they do not let them go, they undergo suffering.

What man of self-control would delight in those passions, which are like fierce raging serpents ? The uncontrolled, when bitten by them in the heart, go to destruction and obtain no relief.

What self-controlled man would delight in those passions, which are like skeletons of dry bones ? Even if they enjoy them, like famished dogs eating a bone, men are not satisfied.

What self-controlled man would delight in those passions, which are like an exposed bait ? Since they are held in joint tenancy with kings, thieves, fire and water, they originate suffering.

What self-controlled man would delight in those passions, which are like dangerous haunts ? By abiding in them there is misfortune on all sides at the hands of one's enemy and of one's relations as well.

What self-controlled man would delight in those passions, which are like fruit hanging on the topmost boughs of a tree ? On the mountains, in the forest, on the rivers, on the sea, men precipitate themselves after them and thereby come to ruin.

What self-controlled man would delight in those passions, which are like the enjoyments of a dream ? Acquired at the price of many bitter efforts, they are lost in this world in a moment.

What self-controlled man would delight in those passions, which are like trenches full of red-hot charcoal ? Though men procure them, increase them, guard them, yet they find no comfort in them.

What self-controlled man would delight in those passions, which are like the knives and fuel-wood of slaughter-houses ? For their sake the Kurus, the Vrsni-Andhakas and the Mekhala-Dandakas went to destruction.

What self-controlled man would delight in those passions, which dissolve friendship ? On their account the Asuras, Sunda and Upasunda, were involved in a mutual feud and perished.

What self-controlled man would delight in those passions, inauspicious and ever inimical as they are ? For their sake men deliver their bodies up to water and fire and wild beasts in this world.

For the passions' sake the ignorant man behaves wretchedly and incurs the suffering of death, bonds and the like. For the passions' sake the living world, made wretched by expectation and tormented, goes to toil and death.

For deer are lured to their destruction by songs, moths fly into the fire for its brightness, the fish greedy for the bait swallows the hook; therefore the objects of sense breed calamity.

But as for the idea that the passions are enjoyments, none of them are reckoned to be enjoyments; for the material objects of sense such as clothes and the like are to be held as merely remedies against suffering in the world.

For water is desired for allaying thirst; food similarly for destroying hunger, a house for protection against wind, sun and rain, and clothing for a covering of the privy parts or against cold.

Similarly a bed is for riddance of drowsiness; thus too a carriage for avoidance of road-fatigue ; thus too a seat for relief from standing, and bathing as a means of cleanliness, health and strength.

Therefore the objects of sense are means for remedying people's Suffering, not enjoyments ; what wise man engaged in a remedial process would assume that he is partaking of enjoyments?

For he who, burning with a bilious fever, should decide that cold treatment was enjoyment, even he, when engaged in a remedial process, would have the idea that the passions were enjoyment.

And since there is nothing absolute in the pleasures, therefore I do not entertain with regard to them the idea of enjoyment; for the very states which show pleasure bring in their turn suffering also.

For warm clothes and aloewood, are pleasant in the cold and unpleasant in the heat; the rays of the moon and sandalwood are pleasant in the heat and unpleasant in the cold.

Since the pairs, gain and loss, etc., are attached to everything in the world, therefore there is no man on earth who is absolutely happy or absolutely miserable.

When I see how intermingled are the natures of pleasure and suffering, I deem kingship and slavery to be alike; for a king is not ever happy, nor a slave always in distress.

As for the argument that in sovereignty there is great authority, it is from this very fact that a king has great suffering; for a king, like a carrying-pole, endures toil for the sake of the world.

"For if a ruler relies on his sovereignty, which is transitory and has many enemies, he is ruined ; or if he does not trust in it, what then is the happiness of a king, who is always trembling with fright ?

And seeing that, even after conquering the whole earth, only one city can serve him as a residence, and in that too only one palace be occupied, surely kingship is but weariness for others' sake.

A king too can only wear one pair of garments and similarly take only a certain measure of food to still his hunger ; so he can only use one bed, only one seat. The other luxuries of a king lead only to the intoxication of pride.

And if you seek to justify this enjoyment on the ground of contentment, I am content without a kingdom and, when a man is contented in the world, are not all luxuries indifferent to him ?

Therefore I, who have set out on the auspicious, peaceful road, am not to be led away towards the passions. But if you bear our friendship in mind, say to me again and again, " Most certainly hold to your vow ".

For I have not entered the forest because of anger nor have I cast aside my diadem because of enemy arrows, nor have I set my ambitions on loftier enjoyments, that I decline this proposal of yours.

For he, who, after letting go a malignant snake, whose nature it is to bite, or a blazing grass torch, whose nature it is to scorch, would decide to catch hold of it again, only he would, after giving up the passions, resort to them again.

Only such a man as having eyesight would envy the blind, or being free the prisoner, or being wealthy the destitute, or being sound in mind the maniac, only he would envy the man given up to the objects of sense.

And it is not right, just because he subsists on alms, to pity the wise man who desires to pass beyond the danger of old age and death, who has the supreme pleasure of religious peace in this life and for whom suffering in the life beyond is abolished.

But pity should be felt for him who, though placed in the height of sovereignty, is overcome by desire, and who does not win the pleasure of religious peace in this life and is subjected to suffering in the life beyond.

But it was worthy of your character, conduct and family to make such a proposal, and so too it befits my character, conduct and family, that I should keep my vow.

For I have been transfixed by the arrow of the cycle of existence and have left my home in order to obtain tranquillity. I would not wish to win a kingdom free from all drawbacks even in the triple heaven, how much less than one in the world of men ?

But as for what you said to me, O king, about the pursuit of the three objects of life in their entirety, that they are the supreme end of man, my doctrine on this point is that they are calamity too ; for the three objects are transitory and fail also to satisfy.

But I deem the highest goal of a man to be the stage in which there is neither old age, nor fear, nor disease, nor birth, nor death, nor anxieties, and in which there is not continuous renewal of activity.

As for your saying that old age should be awaited and that youth is liable to alteration of mind, this is not a fixed rule; for in practice it is seen to be uncertain, old age too may be volatile and youth constant.

But seeing that Death drags the world away against its will at all stages of life, ought the wise man, who desires religious peace, to wait for old age, when the hour of his destruction is not certain ?

Seeing that Death stands like an ill-omened hunter, with old age for his weapon, and scattering the arrows of disease, as he strikes down like deer the people, who dwell in the forests of fate, what illusion can there be about the prolongation of one's days ?

Therefore whether a man be in the prime of life or old or a child, he should haste so to act that, purified in soul and endowed with *dharma,* he may come into possession of the desired continuance or cessation of activity.

And as for your saying that for the sake of *dharma I* should carry out the sacrificial ceremonies which are customary in my family and which bring the desired fruit, I do not approve of sacrifices; for I do not care for happiness which is sought at the price of others' suffering.

For it does not befit the man of compassionate heart to kill another being, who is helpless, out of a desire for a profitable outcome, even though the fruit of the sacrifice should be permanent; how much less should one act thus, when the fruit is transitory ?

And if the true *dharma* were not a different rule of life to be carried out by vows, moral restraint, or quietude, nevertheless it would still be wrong to practise sacrifice, in which the fruit is described as attained by killing another.

That happiness even, which accrues to a man, while still existing in the world, through hurt to another, is not agreeable to a wise compassionate man; how much more so that which is beyond his sight in another existence?

And I am not to be seduced into continuance of activity for future reward. My mind, O king, takes no joy in the spheres of existence; for continuance of activity extends to all forms of rebirth and is uncertain in its effects, just as creepers, struck by rain from a cloud, wave unsteadily in all directions.

And therefore I have come here because I wish to see the sage Arada, who teaches salvation; and I am starting this very day. Good fortune be yours, O king, and bear patiently with my words, which sound harsh in their truth.

Be happy like Indra, shine ever like the sun, flourish with your virtues, understand the highest good in this world, rule the earth, obtain long life, protect the sons of the good with the Aryas, and enter into the glories of sovereignty, O king, observe your own *dharma.*

Just as when rain is produced from the clouds which originate from the smoke, the sign of fire, which is the enemy of cold, then the twice-born fire is freed from its external appearance, so do you liberate your mind on the occasion of the slaughter of the enemies of the destruction of *tamas*, which is the opponent of the sun, the foe of cold."

The king clasped his hands and spoke with eager longing, " May you succeed without hindrance in accordance with your desires ! And when you have in due course obtained the accomplishment of your task, be pleased to show me too your favour."

He made a firm promiae to the king accordingly and then set out for the Vaisvamtara hermitage. The king also looked up at him with amaze, as he wandered on, and then returned to the city of Girivraja.

12

VISIT TO ARADA

Then the moon of the Iksvaku race proceeded to the hermitage of Arada, the sage who dwelt in holy peace; and he filled it, as it were, with his beauty.

As aoon as the sage of the Kalama *gotra* saw him from afar, he called out aloud " Welcome" ; and the prince came up to him.

In accordance with propriety each enquired after the other's health, and then they sat down on pure wooden seats.

The best of sages, drinking in, as it were, the seated prince with eyes opened wide in reverence, said to him :—

" It is known to me, fair sir, how you have come forth from the palace, riving asunder the bonds of family affection, as a savage elephant rives his hobbles.

In every way your mind is steadfast and wise, in that you have abandoned sovereignty, as if it were a creeper with poisonous fruit, and have come here.

No cause for wonder is it that kings, grown old in years, have gone to the forest, giving their children the sovereignty, like a garland that has been worn and is left lying as useless.

But this I deem a wonder that you, who are in the flush of youth and are placed in the pasture-ground of sensory pleasures, should have come here without even enjoying sovereignty.

Therefore you are a fit vessel to grasp this, the highest *dharma*. Go up into the boat of knowledge and quickly pass over the ocean of suffering.

Although the doctrine is only taught after an interval of time, when the student has been well tested, your depth of character and your resolution are such that I need not put you to an examination."

The bull of men, on hearing this speech of Arada, was highly gratified and said to him in reply:–

"The extreme graciousness, which you show me in spite of your freedom from passion, makes me feel as if I had already reached the goal, though it is yet unattained by me.

For I look on your system, as one who wants to see lokks on a light, one who wants to travel on a guide or one who wants to cross a river on a boat.

Therefore you should explain it to me, if you think it right to do so, that this person may be released from old age, death and disease."

Arada, spurred on through the prince's loftiness of soul, described briefly the conclusions of his doctrine thus:—

"Listen, best of listeners, to our tenets, as to how the cycle of life develops and how it ceases to be.

Do you, whose being is steadfast, grasp this : primary matter, secondary matter, birth, death and old age, these, and no more, are called "the being."

But in that group know, O knower of the nature of things, that primary matter consists of the five elements, the ego-principle, intellect and the unseen power.

Understand that by secondary matter is meant the objects of the senses, the senses, the hands and feet, the voice, the organs of generation and excretion, and also the mind.

And that which is conscious is called the knower of the field, because it knows this field. And those who meditate on the *atman* say that the *atman* is the knower of the field.

And awareness is intellectual, that is, Kapila and his pupil in this world. But that which is without intellect is called Prajapati with his sons in this world.

The "seen" is to be recognised as that which is born, grows old, suffers from disease and dies, and the unseen is to be recognised by the contrary.

Wrong knowledge, the power of the act and desire are to be known as the causes of the cycle of existence. The individual person, which abides in these three, dogs not pass beyond that "being".

By reason of misunderstanding, of wrong attribution of personality, of confusion of thought, of wrong conjunction, of lack of discrimination, of wrong means, of attachment, of falling away.

Now of these misunderstanding acts topsy-turvily. It does wrongly what has to be done, it thinks wrongly what it has to think.

But, O prince free from all egoism, wrong attribution of personality shows itself in this world thus, by thinking, "It is I who speak, I who know, I who go, I who stand"

But, O prince free from doubt, that is called in this world confusion of thought which sees as one, like a lump of clay, things which are not mixed up together.

Wrong conjunction means thinking that the ego is identical with this, namely mind, intellect and act, and that this group is identical with the ego.

That is said to be lack of discrimination, which does not know, O knower of the distinctions, the distinction between the intelligent and the unintelligent or between the primary constituents.

Wrong means, O knower of the right means, are declared by the wise to be the use of the invocations *namas* and *vasat*, the various kinds of ritual sprinkling, etc.

O prince free from attachment, attachment is recorded as that through which the fool is attached to the objects of sense by mind, voice, intellect and action.

Falling away is to be understood as wrong imagination about suffering that " this is mine ", "I belong to this ", and thereby a man is caused to fall away in the cycle of transmigration.

For thus that wise teacher declares ignorance to be five-jointed, namely torpor, delusion, great delusion and the two kinds of darkness.

Of these know torpor to be indolence, and delusion to be birth and death, but great delusion, O prince free from delusion, is to be understood as passion.

And because even mighty beings become deluded over this passion, therefore, O hero, it is recorded as great delusion.

And darkness they refer to, O angerless one, as anger, and blind darkness they proclaim, O undesponding one, to be despondency.

The fool, conjoined with this five-jointed ignorance, passes on from birth to birth through the cycle of transmigration which for the greatest part is suffering.

Thus believing that he is the seer and the hearer and the thinker and the instrument of the effect, he wanders in the cycle of transmigration.

Through the action of these causes, O wise one, the stream of birth flows in this world. You should recognise that, when the cause does not come into being, the result does not come into being.

In that matter, O prince desiring salvation, the man of right knowledge should know the group of four, the intelligent, that which lacks intelligence, the seen and the unseen.

For when the knower of the field properly discriminates these four, it abandons the rushing torrent of birth and death, and obtains the everlasting sphere.

For this purpose the Brahmans in the world, who follow the doctrine of the supreme Absolute, practise here the *brahman-course* and instruct the Brahmans in it."

The king's son, on hearing this speech of the sage, questioned him both about the means to be adopted and about the sphere of final beatitude :—

"Deign to explain to me how this *brahman-course* is to be practised, for how long and where, and also where this *dharma* ends."

Arada explained to him concisely by another method the same *dharma* in clear language and according to the *sastra:*—

"The aspirant, after first leaving his family and assuming the mendicant's badges, takes on himself a rule of discipline which covers all proper behaviour.

Displaying entire contentment with whatever he gets from whatever source, he favours a lonely dwelling and, free from the pairs of worldly life, he studies the *sastra* diligently.

Then, seeing the danger that arises from passion and the supreme happiness derived from passionlessness, he arrests his senses and exerts himself in the matter of mental quietude.

Then he wins the first trance, which is dissociated from the loves, malevolence and the like, which is born of discrimination and which includes thought.

And when the fool obtains that transic bliss and reflects on it repeatedly, he is carried away by the gain of previously unexperienced bliss.

Deceived by the feeling of content, he wins to the world of Brahma by means of quietude of this kind, which rejects love and hatred.

But the wise man, knowing that the thoughts cause agitation of mind, obtains the trance, which is disjoined from it and which possesses ectasy and bliss.

He, who is carried away by that ecstasy and does not see any stage superior to it, obtains a station of light among the Abhasvara deities.

But he, who dissociates his mind from the joy of that ecstasy, gains the third trance which is blissful but void of ecstasy.

But he who, immersed in this bliss, does not strive for progress, attains bliss in common with the Subhakrtsna deities.

He who, on attaining such bliss, is indifferent and feels no desire for it, wins the fourth trance, which is void of bliss and suffering.

Some in that trance through vain imagination conclude that it is liberation, because bliss and suffering are abandoned and the mind ceases to function.

But those who investigate the transic knowledge of the Absolute describe its fruit as enduring for many ages with the Brhatphala deities.

On emerging from that concentrated meditation, the wise man sees the evils that exist for those who have a body and betakes himself to knowledge for the cessation of the body.

Then, abandoning the practice of that trance, the wise man sets his mind on progress and turns away from all desire for material form even, as previously from the passions.

First he forms a mental conception of the empty spaces which exist in this body and then he obtains a clear idea of space with regard to its solid matter also.

But another wise man, contracting his self which has extended over space, looks on that very thing as unlimited and reaches a higher stage.

But another, skilled in regard to the inner self, causes his self to cease by his self and, since he sees that there is nothing, he is declared to be one for whom nothing exists.

Then like the *munja* stalk from its sheath or the bird from its cage, the knower of the field, escaped from the body, is declared to be liberated.

This is that supreme Absolute, without attribute, everlasting and immutable, which the learned men who know the principles call liberation.

Thus I have fully shown to you the means and the liberation ; if you have understood it and if it pleases you, undertake it properly.

For Jaigfsavya and Janaka and Vrddha Parasara and other seekers after liberation have been liberated by following this path."

But the prince, marking these words and pondering on them, thus made reply, since he was filled with the force of the motives perfected in previous births :—

"I have listened to this doctrine of yours, which grows more subtile and auspicious in its successive stages, but I consider it not to lead to final beatitude, since the field-knower is not abandoned.

For I am of opinion that the field-knower, although liberated from the primary and secondary constituents, still possesses the quality of giving birth and also of being a seed.

For although the soul by reason of its purity is conceived as being liberated, it will again become bound from the continued existence of the causal conditions.

Just as a seed does not grow for want of the proper season, soil or water, but does grow when these causal conditions are present, such I deem to be the case of the soul.

And as for the statement that liberation is deemed to come by severance from the power of the act, from ignorance and from desire, there is no complete severance from them so long as the soul persists.

It is true that advance is obtained by the progressive abandonment of these three, but where the soul still remains, there these three remain in a subtile state.

But such liberation is a creation of the imagination based on the subtility of the faults, the inactivity of the mind and the length of life in that state.

And as for this imagined abandonment of the ego-principle, so long as the soul persists, there is no abandonment of that principle.

And as the soul is not released from the activity of reason and the like, it is not devoid of attribute; therefore, as it is not devoid of attribute, it is not admitted to be liberated.

For no distinction exists between the attributes and the possessor of the attributes ; for instance, fire is not perceived, when devoid of outward appearance and heat.

Before a conglomerate mass exists, there cannot be a possessor of the mass ; so, before attributes exist, there cannot be a possessor of the attributes. Therefore the soul, as possessor of the body, being first released, is subsequently bound to it again.

And the knower of the field, when without a body, must be either knowing or unknowing. If it is knowing, there is something for it to know, and if there is something for it to know, it is not liberated.

Or if your teaching is that it is unknowing, what then is the use of inventing the existence of a soul ? For even without a soul the existence of the quality of not-knowing is well established as in the case of a log or a wall.

But since this successive abandonment is declared to be meritorious, therefore I deem complete success in reaching the goal to derive from the abandonment of everything."

Thus he was not satisfied on learning the doctrine of Arada, and, discerning that it was incomplete, he turned away from there.

Thereon in his desire to hear something higher he proceeded to the hermitage of Udraka, but he did not accept his system, because it also involved the tenet of the soul's existence.

For the sage Udraka, knowing the defects of consciousness and unconsciousness, found beyond the way of nothingness a way which was characterised by neither consciousness nor unconsciousness.

And since the conscious and unconscious states have each an object in a subtle condition, therefore he thought that beyond them was the state of neither unconsciousness nor consciousness and fixed his desires thereon.

And since the intellect remains in the same condition, without moving elsewhere, subtile and inert, therefore in that state there is neither consciousness nor unconsciousness.

And since a man returns again to the world, even after reaching that point, therefore the Bodhisattva, desiring to obtain the highest stage, left Udraka.

Then with his mind made up in the search for the supreme good, he departed from that hermitage and betook himself to the hermitage, Nagari by name, of the royal seer Gaya.

Thereon the sage, whose every effort was pure and who delighted in a lonely habitation, took up his dwelling on the pure bank of the Nairanjana river.

Then he saw five mendicants, who had come there before him; they had taken vows on themselves and practised austerities, vaunting themselves of control of the five senses.

The mendicants saw him there and, desiring liberation, approached him, as the objects of sense come to a lordly man, whose good merit has earned him wealth and freedom from disease.

Thereon they served him reverently, abiding as pupils under his orders, and were humble and compliant because of their good training, just as the restless senses serve the mind;

While he undertook extraordinary austerities by starvation, thinking that it might be the method for ending death and birth.

Carrying out many kinds of fasting that are difficult for a man to perform, for six years in his desire for quietude he made his body emaciated.

Yearning to reach the further shore of the cycle of transmigration whose further shore is unbounded, he lived by taking at mealtimes a single jujube fruit, sesamum seed and grain of rice.

Whatever his body lost by reason of these austerities, just so much was made good again through his psychic power.

Emaciated as he was, yet with his glory and majesty unimpaired, he was a source of joy to the eyes of others, as the moon in autumn at the beginning of the bright fortnight is to the night lotuses.

Though he had wasted away, so that only akin and bone remained, with fat, flesh and blood all gone, yet with undiminished depth of soul he shone like the ocean, whose depth never diminishes.

Thereon dreading existence the sage, whose body was clearly tormented to no purpose by pernicious austerities, thus resolved in his longing for Buddhahood :—

" This is not the way of life for passionlessness, for enlightenment, for liberation. That is the sure procedure which I won that time beneath the *jambu* tree.

Nor can that be obtained by one who is weak." So in all seriousness he pondered further on this point in order to increase his bodily strength.

How can the result to be attained by the mind be reached by a man, who is not calmly at ease and who is so worn out with the exhaustion of hunger and thirst that his mind is unbalanced with the exhaustion ?

Inward tranquillity is rightly gained by constant appeasement of the senses, and from the full appeasement of the senses the mind becomes well-balanced.

The man whose mind is well-balanced and serene develops concentrated meditation ; when the mind is possessed of concentrated meditation, the practice of trance begins.

By the practice of trance those *dharmas* are obtained, through which is won that highest, peaceful stage, so hard to reach, which is ageless and deathless.

Accordingly the steadfast seer of unbounded wisdom concluded that this method was based on the eating of food and made up his mind to take food.

He bathed and, as in his emaciation he came painfully up the bank of the Nairanjana, the trees growing on the slope bent low the tips of their branches in adoration to give him a helping hand.

At that time on divine instigation Nandabala, the daughter of the cowherd chief, went there, joy bursting from her heart.

She was wearing a dark-blue cloth and her arms were brilliant with white shells, so that she seemed like Yamuna, best of rivers, when its dark-blue water is wreathed with foam.

Her delight was enhanced by faith, and her blue-lotus eyes opened wide, as, doing obeisance with her head, she caused him to accept milk rice.

By partaking of it he secured for her the full reward of her birth and himself through the satisfaction of the six sense faculties became capable of obtaining enlightenment.

Then the sage's form together with his fame reached full roundness and he bore united in his single person the loveliness of the moon and the steadfastness of the ocean.

The five mendicants, holding that he had renounced the holy life, left him, as the five elements leave the thinking soul when it is liberated.

On this with his resolution for sole companion, he made up his mind for enlightenment and proceeded to the root of a *pipal* tree, where the ground was carpeted with green grass.

Then at that moment Kala, the best of serpents, whose might was as that of the king of elephants, was awakened by the incomparable sound of his feet, and, realising that the great sage had determined on enlightenment, he uttered this eulogy :—

"Since, O sage, the earth thunders, as it were, again and again, as it is pressed by your feet, and since your splendour shines forth as of the sun, certainly you will to-day enjoy the desired result.

Since, O lotus-eyed one, the flocks of blue jays, circling in the air, proceed round you right-handed, and since gentle breezes blow in the sky, to-day without doubt you will become a Buddha."

Then, after the lordliest of serpents had thus extolled him, he took clean grass from a grass-cutter, and, betaking himself to the foot of the great pure tree, he made a vow for enlightenment and seated himself.

Then he took up the supreme, immoveable cross-legged posture with his limbs massed together like the coils of a sleeping serpent, saying, " I will not rise from this position on the ground till I achieve the completion of my task ".

Then when the Holy One took his seat with determined soul, the denizens of the heavens felt unequalled joy, and the birds and the companies of wild beasts refrained from noise nor did the forest trees, when struck by the wind, rustle at all.

13

DEFEAT OF MARA

When the great sage, the scion of a line of royal seers, sat down there, after making his vow for liberation, the world rejoiced, but Mara, the enemy of the good Law, trembled.

Him whom in the world they call the God of Love, him of the bright weapon and also the flower-arrowed, that same one, as the monarch of the activities of the passions and as the enemy of liberation, they style Mara.

His three sons, Caprice, Gaiety and Wantonness, and his three daughters. Discontent, Delight and Thirst, asked him why he was depressed in mind, and he answered them thus :—

"The sage, wearing the armour of his vow and drawing the bow of resolution with the arrow of wisdom, sits yonder, desiring to conquer my realm; hence this despondency of my mind.

For if he succeeds in overcoming me and expounds to the world the path of final release, then is my realm to-day empty, like that of the Videha king, when he fell from good conduct.

While therefore he has not yet attained spiritual eyesight and is still within my sphere, I shall go to break his vow, like the swollen current of a river breaking an embankment."

Then, seizing his flower-made bow and his five world-deluding arrows, he, the causer of unrest to mortal minds, approached the *asvattha* tree accompanied by his children.

Next Mara placed his left hand on the tip of the bow and, fingering the arrow, thus addressed the sage, who was tranquilly seated in his desire to cross to the further shore of the ocean of existence :—

"Up, up, Sir Ksatriya, afraid of death. Follow your own *dharma,* give up the *dharma* of liberation. Subdue the world both with arrows and with sacrifices, and from the world obtain the world of Vasava.

For this is the path to issue forth by, the famous one travelled by kings of olden time. It is ignominious for one born in a renowned family of royal seers to practise this mendicancy.

Or if, O firm in purpose, you do not rise up to-day, be steadfast, do not give up your vow. For this arrow that I have ready is the very one I discharged at Surpaka, the fishes' foe.

And at the mere touch of it the son of Ida, though he was the grandson of the moon, fell into a frenzy, and Santanu lost his self-control. How much more then would anyone else do so, who is weak with the decadence of the present age?

So rise up quickly and recover your senses; for this ever-destructive arrow stands ready. I do not discharge it at those who are given to sensual pleasures and show compliance to their mistresses, any more than I would at sheldrakes."

Despite these words the sage of the Sakyas showed no concern and did not change his posture; so then Mara brought forward his sons and daughters and discharged the arrow at him.

But even when the arrow was shot at him, he paid no heed to it and did not falter in his firmness. Mara, seeing him thus, became despondent and, full of anxiety, said softly to himself :—

"When Sambhu, god as he was, was pierced with this arrow, he became agitated with love towards the mountain-king's daughter. That very arrow causes this man no feeling. Is it that he has no heart or that this is not that arrow ?

Therefore he is no fit subject for my flower-arrow or for my excitation or for the application of sexual delight; he merits threats, revilings and blows at the hands of my troops of awe-inspiring spirits."

Then as soon as Mara thought of his army in his desire to obstruct the tranquillity of the SSakya sage, his followers stood round him, in various forms and carrying lances, trees, javelins, clubs and swords in their hands;

Having the faces of boars, fishes, horses, asses and camels, or the countenances of tigers, bears, lions and elephants, one-eyed, many-mouthed, three-headed, with pendulous bellies and speckled bellies;

Without knees or thighs, or with knees vast as pots, or armed with tusks or talons, or with skulls for faces, or with many bodies, or with half their faces broken off or with huge visages;

Ashy-grey in colour, tricked out with red spots, carrying ascetics' staves, with hair smoke-coloured like a monkey's, hung round with garlands, with pendent ears like elephants, clad in skins or entirely naked;

With half their countenances white or half their bodies green; some also copper-coloured, smoke-coloured, tawny or black ; some too with arms having an overgarment of snakes, or with rows of jangling bells at their girdles;

Tall as toddy-palms and grasping stakes, or of the stature of children with projecting tusks, or with the faces of sheep and the eyes of birds, or with cat-faces and human bodies;

With dishevelled hair, or with topknots and half-shaven polls, clothed in red and with disordered headdresses, with bristling faces and frowning visages, suckers of the 'vital essence and suckers of the mind.

Some, as they ran, leapt wildly about, some jumped on each other ; while some gambolled in the sky, others sped along among the treetops.

One danced about, brandishing a trident; another snorted, as he trailed a club; one roared like a bull in his excitement, another blazed fire from every hair.

Such were the hordes of fiends who stood encompassing the root of the *bodhi* tree on all sides, anxious to seize and to kill, and awaiting the command of their master.

Beholding in the beginning of the night the hour of conflict between Mara and the bull of the Sakyas, the sky lost its brightness, the earth shook and the quarters blazed and crashed.

The wind raged wildly in every direction, the stars did not shine, the moon was not seen, and night spread forth still thicker darkness and all the oceans were troubled.

And the earth-bearing Nagas, devoted to *dharma,* did not brook obstruction to the great sage and, turning their eyes wrathfully on Mara, they hissed and unwound their coils.

But the divine sages of the Pure Abodes, absorbed in the fulfilment of the good Law, developed compassion for Mara in their minds, but were untouched by anger, because they were freed from all passion.

When those who were given to *dharma* and desired the liberation of the world saw the root of the *bodhi* tree beset by Mara's cruel host, they raised cries of " Ha ! Ha ! " in the sky.

But when the great seer beheld Mara's army standing as a menace to that method of *dharma,* like a lion seated amidst kine he did not quail nor was he at all perturbed.

Then Mara gave orders to his raging army of demons for terrifying the sage. Thereon that army of his resolved to break down his steadfastness with their various powers.

Some stood trying to frighten him, their many tongues hanging out flickering, their teeth sharp-pointed, their eyes like the sun's orb, their mouths gaping, their ears sticking up stiff as spikes.

As they stood there in such guise, horrible in appearance and manner, he was no more alarmed by them or shrank before them than before over-excited infants at play.

Then one of them, wrathfully turning his gaze on him, raised his club; then his arm with the club became immovable, as was Puramdara's of old with the thunderbolt.

Some lifted up rocks and trees, but were unable to hurl them at the sage. Instead they fell down with the trees and rocks, like the spurs of the Vindhyas when shattered by the levin.

The rocks and trees and axes, discharged by some who flew up into the sky, remained hanging in the air without falling down, like the many-hued rays of the evening clouds.

Another flung above him a blazing log as big as a mountain peak; no sooner was it discharged than, as it hung in the sky, it burst into a hundred fragments through the sage's magic power.

Another, shining like the rising gun, let loose from the sky a vast shower of red-hot coals. just as at the close of the aeon Meru in full conflagration throws out the pulverised scoriae of his golden rifts.

But the shower of hot coals, scattered full of sparks at the foot of the *bodhi* tree, became a shower of red lotus petals through the exercise of universal benevolence on the part of the best of sages.

And the Sakya sage, embracing his resolution like a kinsman, did not waver at all from his posture in spite of these various afflictions and distresses of body and mind, which were cast at him.

Thereon others spat out snake from their mouths as from rotten treetrunks; as if bound by spells, they did not hiss or raise themselves or move in his presence.

Others transformed themselves into huge clouds, accompanied by lightning and the fearsome crash of thunder-stones, and let loose on the tree a shower of stones, which turned into a pleasant rain of flowers.

One too placed an arrow on his bow; it blazed there, but did not shoot forth, like the anger of a poor ill-tempered man, when it is fanned in his heart.

But five arrows shot by another stood arrested in the air and did not fall on the sage, just as, when their objects are present, the five senses of a wise man, who is afraid of the cycle of existence, remain inactive.

Another rushed wrathfully against the great seer, grasping a club in order to kill him; he fell helpless without obtaining his object, as men, not obtaining their desires, fall helplessly into calamitous sins.

But a woman, black as a cloud, with a skull in her hand, wandered about there unrestrainedly and did not remain still, with the intention of deluding the great seer's heart, and resembling the intelligence of a man of inconstant mind wandering uncertainly among the various sacred traditions.

One, wishing to burn him up like a venomous snake with the fire of his glance, levelled a blazing eye on the seer, but failed to see him, as he sat still in the same place, just as a man absorbed in the passions fails to see the true good when it is pointed out to him.

Thus another, lifting a ponderous rock, toiled in vain with his efforts baffled, like one who desires to obtain by affliction of the body the *dharma* which is the ultimate good and which is only to be reached by knowledge and concentration of mind.

Others again, assuming the form of hyenas and lions, loudly roared mighty roars, from which living beings cowered away on every side, thinking the sky had been split by the blow of a thunderbolt.

The deer and the elephants, giving forth cries of distress, ran about and hid themselves, and on that night, as if it were day, the birds on all sides fluttered about, screaming in distress.

But although all beings shivered at such howls of theirs, the sage, like Garuda at the noise of crows, neither trembled nor quailed.

The less the sage was afraid of the fearsome troops of that array, the more was Mara, the enemy of the upholders of the Law, cast down with grief and wrath.

Then a certain being of high station and invisible form, standing in the sky and seeing that Mara was menacing the seer and without cause of enmity was displaying wrath, addressed him with imperious voice :—

"Mara, you should not toil to no purpose, give up your murderous intent and go in peace. For this sage can no more be shaken by you than Meru, greatest of mountains, by the wind.

Fire might lose its nature of being hot, water its liquidity, earth its solidity, but in view of the meritorious deeds accumulated by him through many ages he cannot abandon his resolution.

For such is his vow, his energy, his psychic power, his compassion for creation, that he will not rise up till he has attained the truth, just as the thousand-rayed sun does not rise without dispelling the darkness.

For by rubbing wood long enough a man obtains fire, and by digging the earth deep enough he obtains water; nothing is impossible of achievement to the man of perseverance. Everything that is undertaken by the proper method is thereby necessarily carried out with success.

Therefore since the great physician, in his pity for the world lying distressed in the diseases of passion, etc., toils for the medicine of knowledge, he should not be hindered.

And since the world is being carried away along wrong paths, it is no more proper to harass him, the guide who is laboriously searching for the right path; than it is to harass a good guide, when a caravan has lost its way.

When all beings are lost in the great darkness, he is being made into the lamp of knowledge; it is no more right for your Honour to cause his extinction than it would be to put out a lamp which has been made to shed light in the darkness.

But what honourable man indeed would meditate wrong towards him who, when he sees the world to be drowning in the great flood of the cycle of existence and to be unable to find the further shore, engages himself in ferrying it across?

For the tree of knowledge, when flourishing, should not be cut down, the tree whose fibres are forbearance, which is rooted deep in resolution, whose flowers are good conduct and whose boughs awareness and wisdom, and which yields the fruit of *dharma*.

His purpose is to deliver creation which is bound fast in mind by the snares of delusion. It does not befit you to try to kill him who is exerting himself to deliver mankind from their bondage.

For to-day is the appointed time for the ripening of those deeds which he has done in the past for the sake of illumination. Thus he is seated in this place exactly like the previous sages.

For this is the navel of earth's surface, entirely' possessed of the highest power; for there is no other spot on earth which can bear the force of his concentrated thought.

Therefore be not grieved, calm yourself, Mara, and be not over-proud of your might. Inconstant fortune should not be relied on ; you display arrogance, when your very position is tottering."

And when Mara heard that speech of his and observed the great sage's unshakenness, then, his efforts frustrated, he went away dejectedly with the arrows by which the world is smitten in the heart.

Then his host fled away in all directions, its elation gone, its toil rendered fruitless, its rocks, logs and trees scattered everywhere, like a hostile army whose chief has been slain by the foe.

As he of the flower-banner fled away defeated with his following, and the great seer, the passion-free conqueror of the darkness of ignorance, remained victorious, the heavens shone with the moon like a maiden with a smile, and there fell a rain of sweet-smelling flowers filled with water.

14

ENLIGHTENMENT

Then, after conquering Mara's host by his steadfastness and tranquillity, he, the master of trance, put himself into trance in order to obtain exact knowledge of the ultimate reality.

And after winning entire control over all the methods of trance, he called to mind in the first watch the succession of his previous births.

As though living them over again, he recalled thousands of births, that he had been so-and-so in such-and-such a place and that passing out of that life he had come hither.

Then after recalling his birth and death in these various existences, the compassionate one was filled with compassion for all living beings :—

"Truly the world, in abandoning its kinsfolk in this life and yet proceeding to activity in another existence, is without means of rescue and turns round and round like a wheel."

As he thus with resolute soul was mindful of the past, the conviction grew in him that the cycle of existence was as lacking in substance as the pith of a plantain-tree.

But in the second watch he, whose energy had no peer, gained the supreme divine eyesight, being himself the highest of all who possess sight.

Then with that completely purified divine eyesight he beheld the entire world, as it were in a spotless mirror.

His compassionateness waxed greater, as he saw the passing away and rebirth of all creatures according as their acts were lower or higher.

Those living beings whose acts are sinful pass to the sphere of misery, those others whose deeds are good win a place in the triple heaven.

The former are reborn in the very dreadful fearsome hell and, alas, are woefully tormented with sufferings of many kinds.

Some are made to drink molten iron of the colour of fire; others are impaled howling on a redhot iron pillar.

Some, head downwards, are boiled like meal in iron cauldrons; others are miserably broiled on heaps of burning redhot coals.

Some are devoured by fierce horrid dogs with iron teeth, others by the gloating Iron-beaks as if by crows of iron.

Some, exhausted with the burning, long for cool shade and enter like captives the dark sword-leaved forest.

Some have their arms bound and like wood are chopped up with axes; even in this suffering they do not cease to exist, the power of their acts holding back their vital breaths.

The retribution of the act which was committed by them for the cessation of suffering in the hope of obtaining pleasure, is experienced by them against their will in the shape of this suffering.

These did evil for the sake of pleasure and are now exceedingly tormented. What pleasure, even the slightest, does that enjoyment of theirs cause?

The consequences of the foul act, mirthfully carried out by the foul-minded, are reaped by them with lamentations, when the hour of retribution has matured.

If sinners could thus see the fruit of their acts, they would vomit forth hot blood, as if they had been struck in a vital part.

By reason of their various actions arising from th activity of the mind, these other unfortunates are born among the various kinds of animals.

In this state they are miserably slaughtered, even before the eyes of their relatives, for the sake of their flesh, skin, fur or tusks, or out of mutual enmity or mere wantonness.

And powerless and helpless too, tormented by hunger, thirst and exhaustion, those who become oxen or horses are driven along, their bodies wounded with goads.

And those who become elephants are ridden despite their strength by weaklings, who kick them with foot and heel or torment their heads with the ankus.

In this state, though there are other forms of suffering, suffering arises especially from mutual enmity and from subjection to others.

For catching each other mutually, the sky-dwellers are oppressed by sky-dwellers, water-dwellers by those who move in the water, and land-dwellers by land-dwellers.

And so those, who are obsessed by stinginess, are reborn in the dark world of the Pretas and reap their reward in wretchedness.

With mouths small as the eye of a needle and bellies vast as mountains, their lot is suffering and they are tortured with the sufferings of hunger and thirst.

For reaching the limit of longing, yet kept in existence by their own deeds, they do not succeed in swallowing even the filth thrown away by others.

If man knew that such was the fruit of avarice, he would always give away even the limbs of his own body, as Sibi did.

These other creatures take form again in the filthy hell-like pool called the womb and experience suffering amongst men.

At the first even at the moment of birth they are gripped by sharp hands, as if sharp swords were piercing them, whereat they weep bitterly.

They are loved and cherished and guarded by their kindred who bring them up with every care, only to be defiled by their own various deeds as they pass from suffering to greater suffering.

And in this state the fools, obsessed with desire, are borne along in the ever-flowing stream, thinking all the more, 'this is to be done and this is to be done '

These others, who have accumulated merit, are born in heaven, and are terribly burned by the flames of sensual passion, as by a fire.

And from there they fall, still not satiated with the objects of sense, with eyes turned upwards, their brilliance gone, and wretched at the fading of their garlands.

And as their lovers fall helplessly, the Apsarases regard them pitifully and catch their clothes with their hands.

Some look as if they were falling to earth with their ropes of pearls swaying, as they try to hold up their lovers falling miserably from the pavilions.

Others, wearing ornaments and garlands of many kinds and grieved at their fall into suffering, follow them with eyes unsteady with sympathy.

In their love for those who are falling, the troops of Apsarases beat their breasts with their hands and, distressed, as it were, with great affliction, remain attached to them.

The dwellers in Paradise fall distressed to earth, lamenting, " Alas, grove of Caitraratha ! Alas, heavenly lake ! Alas, Mandakini! Alas, beloved ! "

Seeing that Paradise, obtained by many labours, is uncertain and transitory, and that such suffering will be caused by separation from it,

Alas, inexorably this is in an especial degree the law of action in the world ; this is the nature of the world and yet they do not see it to be such.

Others, who have disjoined themselves from sensual passion, conclude in their minds that their station is eternal; yet they fall miserably from heaven.

In the hells is excessive torture, among animals eating each other, the suffering of hunger and thirst among the pretas, among men the suffering of longings,

In the heavens that are free from love the suffering of rebirth is excessive. For the ever-wandering world of the living there is most certainly no peace anywhere.

This stream of the cycle of existence has no support and is ever subject to death. Creatures, thus beset on all sides, find no resting-place.

Thus with the divine eyesight he examined the five spheres of life and found nothing substantial in existence, just as no heartwood is found in a plantain-tree when it is cut open.

Then as the third watch of that night drew on, the best of those who understand trance meditated on the real nature of this world :—

"Alas ! Living creatures obtain but toil; over and over again they are born, grow old, die, pass on and are reborn.

Further man's sight is veiled by passion and by the darkness of delusion, and from the excess of his blindness he does not know the way out of this great suffering."

After thus considering, he reflected in his mind, " What is it verily, whose existence causes the approach of old age and death ?"

Penetrating the truth to its core, he understood that old age and death are produced, when there is birth.

He saw that head-ache is only possible when the head is already in existence ; for when the birth of a tree has come to pass, then only can the felling of it take place.

Then the thought again arose in him, " What does this birth proceed from ? " Then he saw rightly that birth is produced from existence due to the power of the act.

With his divine eyesight he saw that active being proceeds from the act, not from a Creator or from Nature or from a self or without a cause.

Just as, if the first knot in a bamboo is wisely cut, everything quickly comes into order, so his knowledge advanced in proper order.

Thereon the sage applied his mind to determining the origin of existence. Then he saw that the origin of existence was to be found in appropriation.

This act arises from appropriating the various vows and rules of life, sensual pleasures, views of self and false views, as fire arises by appropriating fuel.

Then the thought occurred to him, "From what cause does appropriation come ?" Thereon he recognised the causal condition of appropriation to lie in thirst.

Just as the forest is set ablaze by a little fire, when the wind fans it, so thirst gives birth to the vast sins of sensual passion and the rest.

Then he reflected, " From what does thirst arise ?" Thereon he concluded that the cause of thirst is sensation.

Mankind, overwhelmed by their sensations, thirst for the means of satisfying them; for no one in the absence of thirst takes pleasure in water.

Then he again meditated," What is the source of sensation?" He, who had put an end to sensation, saw also the cause of sensation to be in contact.

Contact is to be explained as the uniting of the object, the sense and the mind, whence sensation is produced, just as fire is produced from the uniting of the two rubbing sticks and fuel.

Next he considered that contact has a cause. Thereon he recognised the cause to lie in the six organs of sense.

The blind man does not perceive objects, since his eye does not bring them into junction with his mind; if sight exists, the junction takes place. Therefore there is contact, when the sense-organ exists.

Further he made up his mind to understand the origin of the six organs of sense. Thereon the knower of causes knew the cause to be name-and-form.

Just as the leaf and the stalk are only said to exist when there is a shoot in existence, so the six organs of sense only arise when name-and-form is in existence.

Then the thought occurred to him, " What is the cause of name-and-form ?" Thereon he, who had passed to the further side of knowledge, saw its origin to lie in consciousness.

When consciousness arises, name-and-form is produced. When the development of the seed is completed, the sprout assumes a bodily form.

Next he considered, "From what does consciousness come into being ? "Then he knew that it is produced by supporting itself on name-and-form.

Then after he had understood the order of causality, he thought over it; his mind travelled over the views that he had formed and did not turn aside to other thoughts.

Consciousness is the causal condition from which name-and-form is produced. Name-and-form again is the support on which consciousness is based.

Just as a boat conveys a man ..., O consciousness and name-and-form are causes of each other.

Just as redhot iron causes grass to blaze and as blazing grass makes iron redhot, of such a kind is their mutual causality.

Thus he understood that from consciousness arises name-and-form, from the latter originate the senses and from the senses arises contact.

But of contact he knew sensation to be born, out of sensation thirst, out of thirst appropriation, and out of appropriation similarly existence.

From existence comes birth, from birth he knew old age and death arise. He rightly understood that the world is produced by the causal conditions.

Then this conclusion came firmly on him, that from the annihilation of birth old age and death are suppressed; that from the destruction of existence birth itself is destroyed; and that existence ceases to be through the suppression of appropriation.

Further the latter is suppressed through the suppression of thirst; if sensation does not exist, thirst does not exist; if contact is destroyed, sensation does not come into existence; from the non-existence of the six organs of sense contact is destroyed.

Similarly if name-and-form is rightly suppressed, all the six organs of sense are destroyed too ; and the former is suppressed through the suppression of consciousness, and the latter is suppressed also through the suppression of the factors.

Similarly the great seer understood that the factors are suppressed by the complete absence of ignorance. Therefore he knew properly what was to be known and stood out before the world as the Buddha.

The best of men saw no self anywhere from the summit of existence downwards and came to tranquillity, like a fire whose fuel is burnt out, by the eightfold path of supreme insight, which starts forth and quickly reaches the desired point.

Then as his being was perfected, the thought arose in him, " I have obtained this perfect path which was travelled for the sake of the ultimate reality by former families of great seers, who knew the higher and the lower things ".

At that moment of the fourth watch when the dawn came up and all that moves or moves was not stilled, the great seer reached the stage which knows no alteration, the sovereign leader the state of omniscience.

When, as the Buddha, he knew this truth, the earth swayed like a woman drunken with wine, the quarters shone bright with crowds of Siddhas, and mighty drums resounded in the sky.

Pleasant breezes blew softly, the heaven rained moisture from a cloudless sky, and from the trees there dropped flowers and fruit out of due season as if to do him honour.

At that time, just as in Paradise, *mandarava* flowers, lotuses and water-lilies of gold and beryl fell from the sky and bestrewed the place of the Sakya sage.

At that moment none gave way to anger, no one was ill or experienced any discomfort, none resorted to sinful ways or indulged in intoxication of mind; the world became tranquil, as though it had reached perfection.

The companies of deities, who are devoted to salvation, rejoiced; even the beings in the spheres below felt joy. Through the prosperity of the party that favoured virtue the *dharma* spread abroad and the world rose above passion and the darkness of ignorance.

The seers of the Iksvaku race who had been rulers of men, the royal seers and the great seers, filled with joy and wonder at his achievement, stood in their mansions in the heavens reverencing him.

The great seers of the groups of invisible beings proclaimed his praises with loud utterance and the world of the living rejoiced as if flourishing. But Mara was filled with despondency, as before a great precipice.

Then for seven days, free from discomfort of body, he sat, looking into his own mind, his eyes never winking. The sage fulfilled his heart's desire, reflecting that on that spot he had obtained liberation.

Then the sage, who had grasped the principle of causation and was firmly fixed in the system of impersonality, roused himself, and, filled with great compassion, he gazed on the world with his Buddha-eye for the sake of its tranquillity.

Seeing that the world was lost in false views and vain efforts and that its passions were gross, seeing too that the law of salvation was exceeding subtle, he set his mind on remaining immobile.

Then remembering his former promise, he formed a resolution for the preaching of tranquillity. Thereon he reflected in his mind how there are some persons with great passion and others with little passion.

Then when the two chiefs of the heavenly dwellings knew that the Sugata's mind had taken the decision to preach tranquillity, they were filled with a desire for the world's benefit and, shining brightly, approached him.

As he sat, his aim accomplished by the rejection of sin, and the excellent *dharma* he had seen as his best companion, they lauded him in all reverence and addressed these words to him for the good of the world :—

"Ah ! Does not the world deserve such good fortune that your mind should feel compassion for the creatures ? In the world there exist beings of varied capacity, some with great passion, some with little passion.

O sage, having yourself crossed beyond the ocean of existence, rescue the world which is drowning in suffering, and, like a great merchant his wealth, bestow your excellencies on others also.

There are some people here who, knowing what is to their advantage in this world and hereafter, act only for their own good. But it is hard to find in this world or in heaven one who will be active for the good of the world."

After thus addressing the great seer, they returned to the celestial sphere by the way they had come. After the sage also had pondered on that speech, the decision grew strong in him for the liberation of the world.

At the time for the alms-round the gods of the four quarters presented the seer with begging-bowls; Gautama, accepting the four, turned them into one for the sake of his *dharma*.

Then at that time two merchants of a passing caravan, being instigated thereto by a friendly deity, joyfully did obeisance to the seer with exalted minds and were the first to give him alms.

The sage reflected that Arada and Udraka Ramaputra were the two who had minds capable of accepting the *dharma*, but, when he saw that both had gone to heaven, his thoughts turned to the five mendicants.

Then, wishing to preach tranquillity in order to dispel the darkness of ignorance, as the rising sun the darkness, Gautama proceeded to the blessed city, which was beloved of Bhimaratha, and whose various forests are ornamented by the Varanasi.

Then the sage, whose eye was like a bull's, whose gait like a rutting elephant's, desired to go to the land of Kasi, in order to convert the world, and turning his entire body like an elephant, he fixed his unwinking eyes on the *bodhi* tree.

15

THE WHEEL OF THE LAW

Having fulfilled His task, He was informed with the might of religious tranquillity (*sama*), and proceeded alone, yet as if many accompanied Him. A pious mendicant, seeing Him on the road, folded his hands and thus addressed Him:—

"Inasmuch as You are devoid of attachment and have tamed the horses of the senses, while (abiding) among beings who are subject to attachment and the horses of whose senses still run wild, Your form *(akrti?),* like that of the moon, shows contentment through the sweet-tasting savour *(rasd)* of a new wisdom.

Your steadfast face glows here, You have become master of Your senses, and Your eye is that of a mighty bull; certainly You have succeeded in Your aim. Who is Your guru, Reverend Sir, from whom You have learnt this accomplishment ?"

There at He replied, "No teacher have I. There is none for Me to honour, still less none for Me to condemn. I have obtained Nirvana and am not the same as others. Know Me to be the Originator *(Svayambhu)* in respect of the Law.

Since I have entirely comprehended that which should be comprehended, but which others have not comprehended, therefore I am a Buddha. And since I have overthrown the sins *(klesa)* as if they were foes, know me to be One Whose self is tranquillised (*Samatmaka*).

I, good Sir *(saumya),* am now on the way to Varanasi to beat there the drum of the deathless Law, not for the bliss of renown, nor out of pride, but for the good of My fellow-men who are harassed by suffering.

Of yore, on seeing the world of the living to be in distress, I vowed thus, that, when I had crossed Myself, I would bring the world across, that, when Myself liberated, I would emancipate its inhabitants *(sattva).*

Some in this world, gaining wealth, hold it for themselves alone and thereby come to shame; but for the great man *(mahajana)* whose eyes are open, on acquiring pre-eminent objects *(visesa),* that alone is wealth which he distributes.

When a man is being carried away by a stream, he who, standing on dry land, does not try to pull him out, is no hero; and the man who, finding treasure, does not share it with the poor, is no giver.

It is proper for one in good health to doctor a man overcome by disease with the remedies he has in hand, and it is fitting for a master of the ways *(margapati) to* point out the road he should take to one who is on the wrong road.

Just as, when a lamp is lit, there is by reason of it no access of darkness, so when the Buddha makes His knowledge shine, men do not become a prey to passion.

Just as fire must abide in the wood, wind in the air, and water in the earth, so the Enlightenment of the Sages *(muni)* must take place at Gaya and their preaching of the Law at Kasi,"

Thereon, expressing his admiration below his breath *(upamsu),* he quitted the Buddha and went his way according to his desire, but given over to longing and repeatedly looking back at Him with eyes full of wonderment.

Then in due course the Sage saw the city of Kasi, which resembled the interior of a treasure-house, and which the Bhagirathi and the Varanasi, meeting together, embrace like a woman friend.

Resplendent with power and glory, he came shining like the sun to the Deer Park, where dwelt the great seers among trees resounding with cuckoos' calls.

Then the five mendicants, he of the Kaundinya *gotra,* Mahanaman, Vaspa, Asvajit and Bhadrajit, seeing Him from afar, spoke these words among themselves:—

"Here approaches the mendicant Gautama, who in his

fondness for ease has turned away from asceticism. He is certainly not to be met, nor to be saluted; for he who has resiled from his vow merits no reverence.

Should he however wish to talk with us, by all means enter into conversation with him; for men of gentle blood (*arya*) should certainly do so, whoever may be the guest who arrives."

The Buddha moved towards the sitting mendicants, who had thus laid their plans; and as He drew nearer to them, they broke their agreement.

One of them took His mantle, and similarly another with folded hands accepted His begging-bowl. Another gave Him the proper seat, and similarly the other two presented Him with water for His feet.

Showing Him many attentions in such wise, they all treated Him as their Guru; but, as they did not cease calling Him by His family name, the Holy One in His compassion said to them:—

"O mendicants, do not speak to the venerable Arhat after the former fashion with lack of reverence; for, though I am in truth indifferent to praise and blame, I would turn you away from what has evil consequences *(apunya).*

Seeing that a Buddha obtains Enlightenment for the good of the world, He ever acts for the good of all beings; and the Law is cut off for him who maliciously calls his guru by his name, just as in the case of disrespect to parents."

Thus did the Great Seer, the Best of speakers, preach to them out of the compassion of His heart; but led astray by delusion and lack of ballast (*asarena*), they answered Him with gently smiling faces:—

"You did not forsooth, Gautama, come to an understanding of the real truth by those supreme and excellent austerities, and, though the goal is only to be obtained with difficulty (*krcchrena?*) you indulge in comfort. "What is your ground for saying, 'I have seen'?"

Since the mendicants thus displayed their scepticism regarding the truth about the Tathagata, then the Knower of the Path, knowing the path to Enlightenment to be other than that, expounded the path to them:—

"The fool who tortures himself and equally he who is attached to the domains of the senses, both these you should regard as in fault, because they have taken paths, which do not lead to deathlessness.

The former, with his mind troubled and overcome *(akranta?)* by the bodily toils called austerities, becomes unconscious and does not know even the ordinary course *(vyavahara)* of the world, how much less then the supersensual way of truth ?

Just as in this world one does not pour out water to obtain a light for the destruction of darkness, so bodily torments are not the prerequisite for the destruction of the darkness of ignorance by the fire of knowledge.

Just as a man who wants a fire does not obtain it by boring and splitting wood, but does succeed by using the proper means, so deathlessness is obtained by *yoga,* not by torments.

Similarly those who are attached to the calamitous lusts have their minds overwhelmed by passion *(rajas)* and ignorance *(tamas);* they do not even attain the ability to understand the doctrines *(sastra),* still less then the passionless *(viraga)* method of suppression.

Just as the individual who is overcome by illness is not cured by eating unwholesome food, so how shall he, who is overcome by the disease of ignorance *(ajnana)* and is addicted to the lusts, reach religious peace ?

Just as a fire does not go out, when it has dry grass *(kaksa?)* for fuel *(asraya)* and the wind fans it, so the mind does not come to peace, when passion *(raga)* is its companion and the lusts its support *(asraya).*

Abandoning either extreme, I have won to another, the Middle Path, which brings surcease from sorrow and passes beyond bliss and ecstasy.

The sun of right views illumines it, the chariot of pure right thought fares along it, the rest-houses *(vihara)* are right words rightly spoken, and it is gay with a hundred groves of good conduct.

It enjoys the great prosperity *(subhiksa)* of noble livelihood, and has the army and retinue of right effort; it is guarded on all sides by the fortifications of right awareness and is provided with the bed and seat of concentrated thought.

Such in this world is this most excellent eightfold path, by which comes release from death, old age and disease; by passing along it, all is done that has to be done, and there is no further travelling in this world or the next.

'This is nothing but suffering, this is the cause, this is the suppression and this the path to it (sc. suppression)': thus tor salvation's sake I developed eyesight for an unprecedented method of the Law, which had been hitherto unheard of.

Birth, old age, disease and eke death, separation from what is desired, union with what is not desired, failure to attain the longed for end, these are the varied sufferings that men undergo.

In whatever state a man be existing, whether he is subject to the lusts or has conquered self, whether he has or has not a body, whatever quality *(guna)* is lacking to him, know that in short to be suffering.

It is My settled doctrine that, just as a fire, when its flames die down, does not lose its inborn nature of being hot, however small it be, so the idea of self, subtle though it may become through quietude and the like, has still the nature of suffering.

Recognise that, just as the soil, water, seed and the season are the causes of the shoot *(amkura)*, so the various sins *(dosa)*, passion *(kamaraga)* and the like, as well as the deeds that spring from the sins, are the causes of suffering.

The cause for the stream of existence, whether in heaven or below, is the group of sins, passion and the like; and the root of the distinction here and there into base, middling and high, is the deeds.

From the destruction of the sins the cause of the cycle of existence ceases to be, and from the destruction of the Act that suffering ceases to be; for, since all things come into being from the existence of something else, with the disappearance of that something else they cease to be.

Know suppression to be that in which there is not either birth, or old age, or death, or fire, or earth, or water, or space, or wind, which is without beginning or end, noble and not to be taken away *(aharya),* blissful and immutable.

The path is that which is described as eightfold, and outside it there are no means for success *(adhigama).* Because they do not see this path, men ever revolve *(paribhram)* in the various paths.

Thus I came to the conclusion in this matter, that suffering is to be recognised, the cause to be abandoned, the suppression to be realised and the path to be cultivated.

Thus insight *(caksus)* developed in me that this suffering has been recognised and the cause abandoned, similarly that the suppression has been realised, similarly that this path has been cultivated.

I did not claim to be emancipated in this world and did not see too in Myself the attainment of the goal, so long as I had not seen these four stages of the noble right truth.

But when I had mastered the noble Truths, and, having mastered them, had done the task that was to be done, then I claimed to be emancipated in this matter and saw that I had attained the goal "

When the Great Seer, full of compassion, thus preached the Law there in these words, he of the Kaundinya clan and a hundred deities obtained the insight that is pure and free from passion *(rajas).*

When he had completed all that was to be done, the Omniscient said to him with a voice loud as a bull's, " Is the knowledge yours ?" That great-souled one replied, "Truly *(paramam);* I know Your excellent thought."

Then by saying " Truly, I know," Kaundinya (was the first) in the world to grasp the knowledge of that stage and came into possession of the Law at the head of the mendicants of the holy Guru, the Tathagata.

When the Yaksas, who lived on the earth, heard that cry, they proclaimed with resounding voices, "Most certainly the Wheel of the Law has been well turned by the Best of those who see, for the deathless tranquillity of all beings.

Its spokes are the discipline *(sila)*, its fellows tranquillity *(sama)* and the Rule *(vinaya)*, wide in understanding *(buddhi?)* and firm with awareness *(smrti)* and wisdom *(mati)*, its pin is self-respect *(hri)*. By reason of its profundity, of its freedom from falsehood, and of the excellence of its preaching, it is not overturned by other doctrines when taught in the triple world."

Hearing the shouts of the mountain Yaksas, the troops of deities in the sky took up the cry, and so it mounted loudly from heaven to heaven up to the world of Brahma.

Certain self-controlled *(atmavat)* dwellers in the heavens, on hearing from the Great Seer that the triple world is transitory, desisted from attachment to the various objects of sense, and through their perturbation of mind *(samvega)* reached a state of tranquillity with respect to the three spheres of existence.

At the moment when the Wheel of the Law was thus turned in heaven and earth for the best tranquillity of the three worlds, a shower of rain, laden with flowers, fell from the cloudless sky, and the inhabitants, of the three spheres of existence caused mighty drums to resound.

16

CONVERSION

Then the Omniscient established in the Law of Salvation Asvajit and the other mendicants, who had become well-disposed *(prayata)* in mind.

He appeared surrounded, by that group of five, who had subdued the group of five (senses), like the moon in the sky conjoined with the five stars of the asterism (Hasta) whose regent is the sun.

Now at that time a noble's son named Yasas saw certain women carelessly asleep and thereby became perturbed in mind.

Uttering the words, " How wretched all this is," he went just as he was, retaining all the glory of his magnificent ornaments, to where the Buddha was.

The Tathagata, who knew men's dispositions and sins, on seeing him said, " There is no fixed time for Nirvana, come hither and obtain the state of blessedness."

Hearing these far-famed words, he came, like one entering a river when afflicted with heat, to extreme contentment of mind.

Then by reason of the force of the previous cause, but with his body as it was (i.e. in the householder's garb), he realised Arhatship with body and mind.

As the dye is absorbed by a cloth which has been bleached with salted water, so he, whose mind was white, fully understood the good Law as soon as he heard of it.

The Best of speakers, He who had fulfilled His task and

knew the good goal, saw him standing there ashamed of his clothes and said:—

"The mendicant's badges *(linga)* are not the cause of the Law; he who looks with equal mind on all beings and has restrained his senses by quietude and the Rule, though he wears ornaments, yet walks in the Law.

He who leaves his home with his body, but not with his mind, and who is still subject to passion, is to be known as a householder, though he live in the forest.

He who goes forth with his mind, but not with his body, and who is selfless, is to be known as a forest-dweller, though he abide in his home.

He is said to be emancipated, who has reached this attainment, whether he abide in his home or whether he has become a wandering mendicant.

Just as one who would conquer puts on his armour to overcome a hostile army, a man wears the badges to overcome the hostile army of the sins."

Then the Tathagata said to him," Come hither, mendicant"; and at these words he appeared wearing the mendicant's badges.

Then out of attachment to him his friends, to the number of fifty and three and one, gained the Law.

As garments, covered with potash *(ksara)*, quickly become clean on contact with water, so they quickly became pure, by virtue of their acts having been purified in former ages.

Then at that time sixty in all was the first company of the disciples, who were also Arhats; and the Arhat, fittingly revered by the Arhats, spoke to them as follows:—

"O mendicants, you have passed beyond suffering and fulfilled your great task. It is proper now to help others who are still suffering.

Therefore do all of you, each by himself, traverse this earth and impart the Law to mankind out of compassion for their affliction.

I for *my* part am proceeding to Gaya, the abode of royal

seers, in order to convert the Kasyapa seers, who through their attainments are possessed of supernatural powers."

Then they, who had seen the real truth, departed on His orders in all directions, while the Great Seer, the Blessed One *(Sugata)*, Who was freed from the pairs *(dvandva)*, went to Gaya.

Then in due coarse He arrived there, and, approaching the forest of the Law, saw Kasyapa, abiding there like Asceticism in person.

Although there were dwellings in the mountains and the groves, the Lord of the Ten Powers, desirous of converting him, asked him for a lodging.

Then in order to destroy the Saint *(siddha)*, in his evil disposition *(visamastha)* he gave Him a fire-house, (infested) by a great snake ...

At night the snake, whose gaze was poisonous, saw the Great Sage calm and fearless there looking at him, and in his fury he hissed at Him.

The fire-house was set a light by his wrath, but the fire, as if afraid, did not touch the Great Seer's body.

Just as at the end of the great aeon Brahma shines sitting when the conflagration dies down, so Gautama remained unperturbed, though the fire-house was all blazing.

On the Buddha sitting there, unharmed and moveless, the snake was filled with wonderment and did obeisance to the Best of seers.

The folk in the deer-park thought of the Seer sitting there, and deeply distressed (?) were overcome with pity that such a mendicant should have been burnt.

On the night passing away, the Teacher *(Vinayaka')* took up the snake quietly in His alms-bowl and showed it to Kasyapa.

On perceiving the might of the Buddha, he was amazed, yet be still believed himself to have no superior in power.

Then, as He knew those thoughts of his, the tranquil Sage purified his heart by assuming various shapes suited to the occasion.

Thereon, as he deemed the Buddha to be greater than him in magic power, he determined to win His Law.

The company of A'aruvilva Kasyapa's five hundred followers, seeing his sudden change of heart, adhered also to the Law.

When their brother and his pupils had passed to the further shore *(paraga)* and cast aside their bark garments, the two who were called G-aya and Nadi (Kasyapa) arrived there and betook themselves to the path.

On the Gayasirsa mountain the Sage then preached the sermon of salvation to the three Kasyapa brothers with their followers;—

"The entire world is helplessly burnt up by the fire of love and hate *(ragadvesa)*, which is overspread with the smoke of delusion *(moha)* and originates in the thoughts *(vitarka)*.

Thus scorched by the fire of the sins, without peace or leadership, it is unceasingly consumed again and again by the fires of old age, disease and death.

On seeing this world without refuge and burnt up by manifold fires, the wise man is perturbed over his body with its accompaniment of mind and sense-organs.

From perturbation he proceeds to passionlessness and from that to liberation; thereon being liberated, he knows that he is liberated in all respects.

Having fully examined the stream of birth, he takes his stand on the ascetic life and completes his task; for him there is no further existence."

When the thousand mendicants heard this sermon of the Holy One, by reason of non-appropriation *(anupadana)* their minds were immediately released from the infections *(asrava)*.

Then the Buddha appeared with the three Kasyapas, whose wisdom *(prajna)* was great, like the Law incarnate surrounded by Charity *(dana)*, Discipline and the Rule.

The penance grove, deprived of those excellent..., was no longer brilliant, like the life of a sick man *(sattva), who is* without religion *(dharma)*, wealth or pleasure.

Then remembering His former promise to the Magadha king", the Sage, surrounded by all of them, took His way to Eajagrha.

Then when the king heard of the Tathagata's arrival at the domain of the Venuvana, he went to visit Him, with his ministers in attendance on him.

Then the common folk, with their eyes opened wide in wonderment, came out along the mountain road, on foot or in vehicles? according to their station in life.

On seeing the excellent Sage from afar, the Magadha sovereign hastily alighted from his chariot in order to show Him reverence.

The king left behind him his yaks' tails, his fans and his retinue, and approached the Sage, as Indra approached Brahma.

He did obeisance to the Great Seer with his head so that his headdress shook, and with His permission sat down on the ground on the soft grass.

The thought occurred to the people there, "Oh ! The might of the Sakya Sage. Has the seer, His Holiness Kasyapa, become His pupil ?"

Then the Buddha, knowing their minds, said to Kasyapa, "Kasyapa, what was the quality you saw that you abandoned fire-worship?"

When the Guru thus incited him with a voice like that of a mighty raincloud, he folded his hands and said aloud in the crowded assembly:—

"I have given up the fires, because the fruit of worshipping them and of making oblations in them is continuance in the cycle of existence and association with the various mental ills.

I have given up the fires, because by muttering prayers, offering oblations and the like out of thirst for the objects of sense the thirst for them merely grows stronger.

I have given up the fires, because by muttered prayers and fire-oblations there is no cessation from birth, and because the suffering of birth is great.

I have given up the fires, because the belief that the supreme good comes from rites of worship and from austerities is false.

I have given up the fires, because, as I affirm, I know the blissful immutable stage, which is delivered from birth and death."

On hearing the converted Kasyapa thus speak words, so productive of faith and so full of matter, the Master of the Rule *(Vinaya)* said to him:—

"Hail to you, most noble one *(mahabhaga)*; this is most certainly the good work that you have done, in that among the various Laws you have attained that which is the best.

Just stir up then the hearts of the assembly by displaying your various magic powers, as one will has great possessions displays his various treasures."

Then Kasyapa said, "Very well," and, contracting himself into himself, he flew up like a bird into the path of the wind.

This master of the miraculous powers stood in the sky as on a treestump, walked about as on the ground, sat down as on a couch and then lay down.

Now he blazed like a fire, now he shed water like a cloud, now he blazed and poured forth water simultaneously.

As he took great strides, blazing and shedding water, he appeared like a cloud pouring forth rain and brilliant with flashes of lightning.

The people looked up at him in amazement, with their eyes glued to him, and, as they did obeisance to him in reverence, they uttered lion-roars.

Then, bringing his magic display to a close, he did obeisance to the Sage with his head and said, " I am the pupil who has done his task; my master is the Holy One."

The inhabitants of Magadha, seeing Kasyapa do obeisance to the Great Seer in this fashion, concluded that it was the Blessed One Who was Omniscient.

Then He, Who abode in the supreme good, knew that the soil was prepared and for his welfare said to Srenya, who was desirous of hearing the Law:—.

"O lord of the earth, O thou who art possessed of great majesty and hast control of the senses, Form *(rupa)* is born and decays accompanied by the mind and the senses.

Their birth and passing away should be known for the furtherance of virtue, and, by knowing these two matters correctly, come to a right understanding of the body.

By knowing the body with the senses to be subject to birth and passing away, there is no appropriation at all, no coming to the idea that it is 'I' or 'mine.'

The body and the senses have no objectivity outside the mental conceptions; they are born as suffering, as suffering they pass away.

When all this is understood to be neither 'I' nor 'mine,' then the supreme unchangeable Nirvana is reached.

Through the sins of assuming the existence of the ego and the like men are bound in the false conception of self *(atmagraha)*, and when they see that there is no self, they are released from the passions.

The false view binds, the right view releases; this world, abiding in the thought that there is a self, does not grasp the truth.

If a self did exist, it would be either permanent or impermanent; great defects follow from either alternative.

Just suppose it to be impermanent, then there would be no fruit of the act; and, since there would be no rebirth, salvation would come without effort on our part.

Or if it were permanent and all-pervading, there would be neither birth nor death; for space, which is all-pervading and permanent, neither passes away nor is born.

If this self were all-pervading in nature, there would be no place where it is not; and when it passed away, there would simultaneously *(ca....ca)* be salvation for everyone together.

As being all-pervading by nature, it would be inactive and there would be no doing of the act; and without the doing of acts, how could there be the union with the fruit of them?

It the self did perform deeds, it would cause no suffering to itself; for who, that is his own master, would cause suffering to himself ?

The theory of a permanent self leads to the conclusion that it undergoes no change; but, since it experiences pleasure and suffering, we see that it does incur change.

Salvation conies from the winning of knowledge and the abandonment of sin; and since the self is inactive and all-pervading, there would be no salvation for it.

One should not say this, namely that there is a self, since in reality it has no existence *(asattvabhavat tattvena);* moreover, as having no causal efficiency, it is incapable of any action.

Since then it is not clear what is the work to be done nor by whom it is done, the self cannot be said to exist in such wise (i.e. as either permanent or impermanent), and therefore it has no existence.

Listen, best of listeners, to this teaching—how the stream of the cycle of existence flows along, bearing away this body, in which there is neither one who acts, nor one who experiences sensations *(vedaka),* nor one who directs.

A sixfold consciousness arises based on the six organs of sense and their six objects; a system of contact develops separately for each group of three, whence awareness, volitions and actions come into activity.

Just as, from the conjunction of a burning-glass jewel, fuel and the sun, fire is produced by virtue of the union, even so all actions dependent on the individual take place, based on the consciousness *(buddhi),* the objects of sense and the senses.

Just as the shoot is produced from the seed, and yet the shoot is not to be identified with the seed, norcan either of them exist without the other, on such wise is the body and the interaction *(krama?)* of the senses and the consciousness."

When the Magadha king heard the sermon of the Best of sages, announcing the highest goal, the supreme beatitude, then the eye of the Law grew in him, the eye that is without stain, without equal, and devoid of passion *(rajas)*.

Many men who dwelt in the capital of Magadha and the inhabitants of heaven became pure in mind in that assembly, on hearing the Sage's preaching, and won to the stage where death and change are not.

17

GREAT DISCIPLES

Thereon the king presented to the Sage for His abode the glorious garden of Venuvana, and with His permission returned to the city, entirely changed in being *(dvitiya?)* through his comprehension of the truth.

Then holding up for salvation's sake the auspicious lamp that is produced from knowledge, the Buddha dwelt in the Vihara in company with Brahma, the gods and saintly beings *(arya)* of the various spheres of existence *(vihara?)*.

Then Asvajit, who had broken the horses of his senses in, entered Rajagrha in search of alms, and held the eyes of great crowd by his beauty, his tranquillity and his demeanour.

A mendicant of Kapila's sect, who had many pupils, famed *(prasasta?)* as Saradvatiputra, saw him coming with his senses tranquillised, and, following him on the road, thus addressed him:—

"On seeing your fresh appearance and your tranquillity, my mind is exceedingly amazed. Just tell me therefore if you know the final truth, what is the name of your teacher, what he teaches and who he is."

When the Brahman spoke thus with every mark of respect, Asvajit also said to him, "My Master was born of the Iksvaku race and is omniscient and without peer.

As I am ignorant and only recently born into the Law, I am not capable of explaining the teaching to you. Hear *(nibodha?)* however a small portion of the words of the Great Sage, Who is the Best of those who know how to speak.

The Holy One has explained the causes of all the elements *(dharma)* which arise from causes. He has explained what is the suppression of them and what the means of their suppression."

When the twice-born, whose name was Upatisya, heard these words of Asvajit, straightway his eyes were opened to the Law and became free from passion *(rajas')*, blissful and pure.

Previously he had held the theory that the field-knower *(ksetrajna)* is uncaused, inactive, and the originator *(isvara)*; on hearing that all these things take place in dependence on causes, he perceived that there is no self and saw the supreme truth.

He held that the Samkhya consider the body to consist of parts and therefore only destroys the group of gross sins, but that under the Buddha's teaching gross and subtle are destroyed alike.

When one embraces the idea of the soul *(atman)* as the origin, there is no abandonment of the ego-principle, and therefore no abandonment of the ego. When a lamp and the sun are both present, what is to be known as a cause of the destruction of light ?

Just as if one cuts off the roots of a lotus, the fine fibres remain entangled with one another, so he deemed the (Samkhya) method, of salvation not to lead to finality, while the Buddha's method was like cutting a stone.

Then the Brahman did reverence to Asvajit and himself departed in high contentment to his dwelling, while Asvajit, after completing his alms-round in due order, proceeded soberly and wisely to the Venuvana.

When he who was born in the Maudgala *gotra* and whose actions corresponded to his learning and knowledge saw Upatisya returning thus filled with the highest peace *(prasada)*, he said to him;—

"O mendicant, why being the same have you become like another ? You have returned steadfast and rejoicing. Have you to-day found the deathless state ? Such calm as this is not without a cause."

Then he explained the truth to him, saying " Thus is it done." Then he said, " Tell me the doctrine." Thereon he repeated the same words to him, and on hearing them the right eyesight was produced in him too.

As their minds had been purified by their actions and dispositions (asaya?), they saw the real truth as it were a lamp held in their hands, and since by reason of their knowing it their feelings towards the Teacher were unswerving, they set off at that instant to see him.

The Great Seer, the Holy One, saw from afar these two coming with their company of disciples and said to the mendicants, " These two, coming here, are my chief disciples, the chiefs, the one of those who have wisdom, the other of those who have magic powers."

Then the tranquil Sage in deep and solemn tones addressed His speech to the pair, "O mendicants, who have come hither for the sake of quietude, receive this Law rightly in proper form."

The Brahmans were bearing the triple staff and twisted locks, but in the very moment that the Tathagata uttered these words to them, they were turned by the Buddha's might into mendicants dressed in ochre-coloured robes.

These two, thus habited, with their company of disciples, did obeisance to the Omniscient with their heads. Then, on the Buddha's preaching the Law to them, in due time both reached the final beatitude.

Then a Brahman, the lamp of the Kasyapa clan, who was possessed of colour, beauty and riches, abandoned his wealth and his beautiful wife, and, taking on himself the ochre-coloured robe, went in search of salvation.

He who had given up all his possessions saw by the Bahuputraka Caitya the Omniscient blazing like a sacred flagpole (or, caitya) of the finest gold; and, filled with amazement, he folded his hands and approached Him.

He did obeisance to the Sage from afar with his head, and, having folded his hands, spoke out loud in fitting manner, "I am the disciple, the Holy One is my Master; O Steadfast One, be my light in the darkness."

The Tathagata, the Appeaser of the mind with the water of His word, recognised that the twice-born had come because desire (for knowledge) had been bred in him, and that he was pure in disposition and desirous of salvation; therefore He said to him, " Welcome."

With his weariness relieved, as it were, by these words, he abode there in order to search for the final beatitude. Then, as his nature was pure, the Sage took pity on him and explained the Law to him summarily.

Because, when the Sage merely explained the Law briefly, he arrived entirely at its purport, therefore from his penetration *(pratisamvid?)* and great fame he was called the Arhat Mahakasyapa.

He had held the self *(atman)* to be both "I" and "mine," as being other than the body and yet in the body. He now abandoned that view of self and looked on it as perpetual (?) suffering.

He had sought for purity by discipline and vows *(sila-vrata)*, finding the cause in that which was not a cause; now he had arrived at the nature of suffering and the path, and held discipline and vows not to be the supreme method.

He had wandered on the wrong course and failed to obtain the best; now he saw the stages of the Four Truths and fully cut off doubts and hesitations.

Recognising the impurity and unreality of the lusts, about which the world has been deluded, is deluded and will be deluded, he abandoned the objects of sense known as the passions.

Thus having attained benevolence *(maitri?)* in thought, he made no distinction between friend and foe, and, compassionating all creatures, he was freed too in mind from internal malevolence *(vyapada)*.

He abandoned the ideas *(samjna)*, informed with manifoldness, that are based on matter and the reactions *(pratigha)* to it, and understood the evils that are active in matter; so he overcame attachment to the sphere of matter *(rupadhatu')*.

He recognised that the stage of the Arupa deities, who deem in their delusion that the trances are salvation, is transitory: and becoming tranquil, he achieved the mind that is empty of object *(nimitta)* and gave up attachment to the Arupa existence.

He realised that the restlessness of the mind was a source of disturbance, flowing as it does like the mighty current of a great river *(sindhu),* and abandoning indolence by the help of steadfastness *(dhairya),* he won to quietude and came to a standstill, like a lake that is full.

He saw the states of being *(bhava)* to be without substance *(sara)* or self and to be subject to passing away *(vyaya);* and seeing nothing to be inferior, equal or superior, he put away false self-esteem *(abhimana?)* and held that there was no reality (in the states of being).

Dispelling the darkness of ignorance (ajnana) with the fire of knowledge *(jnana),* he saw the transitory and the permanent to be different, and perfecting his science *(vidya)* by yoga, he duly extirpated delusion *(avidya).*

Conjoined, with insight *(darsana)* and contemplation *(bhavana),* he was released from this group of ten *(samyojanas),* and, his task completed, his soul at rest, he stood regarding the Buddha, with folded hands.

The Blessed One shone with His three disciples, who had the triple knowledge *(traividya),* and who had exhausted the three *(asravas),* and who were in full possession *(adhigama?)* of the three *(sila samadhi, prajna?'),* like the moon when full (lit., in the third *parvan)* and united at the fifteenth *muhurta* with the three-starred asterism (Jyestha), whose regent is the after-born *{anuja}* god (Indra).

18

THE INSTRUCTION OF ANATHAPINDADA

Thereafter at a certain time there came from the north out of the Kosala country a wealthy householder, who was in the habit of giving wealth to the destitute and who was known under the famous name of Sudatta.

He heard that the Sage was abiding there, and having heard he desired to see Him and went to Him at night. He did obeisance to the Blessed One, Who, knowing that he had arrived with his nature purified *(visuddhasattva)*, instructed him:—

"O wise man, since in your thirst for the law you have given up sleep and come to see Me at night, let then the lamp of final beatitude he raised here at once for the man who has thus come *(tathagata)*.

The display of these great qualities is due to your disposition *(adhyasaya)*, to your steadfastness, to your faith on hearing tell of Me, and to the activity of your mind by virtue of the previous cause.

Therefore, knowing that fame in this world and the reward in the hereafter arise from giving the best, you should at the proper time with due honour and devout mind give the treasure that is won through the Law.

Regulate your conduct by taking on yourself the discipline *(sila)*; for discipline, when observed and adorned, removes all danger of the evil spheres of existence below and cannot but raise a man to the heavens above.

Observing the evil consequences, of search, &c. that are involved in the many attachments to the lusts, and realising the good consequences of the way of renunciation, devote yourself to the truth of quietude which is born of discrimination *(viveka).*

Rightly seeing that the world wanders under the affliction of death and the oppression of old age, strive for the quietude that is delivered from birth and that, by not being subject to birth, is devoid of old age and death.

Just as you know that by reason of impermanency suffering ever persists among men, so know that there is the same suffering among the gods. There is no permanence at all in the continuance of active being *(pravrtti).*

Where there is impermanence, there is suffering'; where there is no absolute self, there also is suffering. How then can there be an 'I' or a 'mine' in that which is impermanent, suffering and without self ?

Therefore look on this suffering as the suffering, and the origin of this as the origin, and know the suppression of suffering as the suppression *(vyupasama)* and the auspicious path as the path.

Know this world to be suffering and transitory, and observing mankind to be entirely burnt up with the fire of Time as with a real fire, hold existence and annihilation alike to be undesirable.

Know this world to be empty, without 'I' or 'mine,' like an illusion, and considering this body as merely the product of the factors *(samskara),* think of it as consisting only of the elements.

Shake your mind free from transitory existence; and observing" the various spheres of rebirth *(gati)* in the cycle of existence, educate *(bhavaya)* your mind, so that it is devoid of thought *[vitarka?*), fixed in Quietude and free from passion. Then paractise the 'absence of object' *(animitta)*."

Then on hearing the Law of the Great Seer, he obtained the first fruit of practice of the Law; and by its attainment only one drop remained over from the great ocean of suffering for him.

Though still living in the house, he realised by insight the highest good, the peal truth, which is not for him who has no insight, whether in the grove or in heaven, though he dwell in the forest of those who are free from desire or on the peak of incorporeal existence.

Since they are not released from the meshes of the various false views and from the sufferings of the cycle of existence, they are lost by not seeing the real truth and arrive at a loftier station *(visesa)* merely by being rid of passion.

With the correct view born in him, he shed the wrong views, like an autumnal cloud shedding a shower of stones, and he did not hold that the world proceeded from a wrong cause, such as a Creator *(isvara)* and the like, or that it was uncaused.

For, if the cause is of a different nature (to the effect), there is no birth *(upapatti)*, and (to believe in) the absence of a cause is a great mistake. Seeing these points respectively by bis learning and knowledge, he was certainly free from doubt in his view of the real truth.

If a Creator produced the world, there would be no ordered process of activity in it, and men would not revolve in the cycle of existence; in whatever state of existence anyone was born, there would he remain.

Corporeal beings would not encounter what they did not desire, nor for beings of such a nature would there be any production of what they desire. Whatever good and evil should come for corporeal beings would take place in the Creator for the sake of the Creator himself.

Men would entertain no doubts about the Creator himself and would feel affection for him as for a father. When calamities come on them, they would not speak injuriously of him, nor would the world worship various deities.

If there should be a purpose *(bhava?)* in his creation, then he is not the creator here to-day, as it (sc. the creation) would be the effect of the purpose (not of the Creator); for, if this continued activity of the purpose is asserted, it is that

that would be the cause of there being a Creator.

Or if his creation is not actuated by any intention, his actions are causeless like a child's, and if the Creator has no dominion over himself, what power can he have to create the world ?

If he causes beings in the world to feel pleasure and suffering according to his desires, then, since thereby attachment to, or aversion from, the object takes place in him, the dominion does not reside in him (but in the objects).

Men would stand under his control without will of their own, and his would be the responsibility for their efforts. There would be nothing done by the corporeal being and no fruit of the act; junction with the act *{karmayoga)* would depend on him.

If it is his actions that make him the Creator, then (since his actions are shared in common with men) he would not be the Creator. Or if he is all-pervading *(vibhu)* and without cause, then the Creatorship of the whole world would be established.

Or if there is any action other than that of the Creator, by reason of that very fact there would be an efficient Creator other than him, and it is not agreed *(avyavasthita)* that there is any (creator) other than him; therefore there is no creator of the world.

He saw the many kinds of contradiction that arise from the conception of Isvara as the Creator, and therefore also the same defects are inherent in the theory of Nature.

The latter view denies to some extent the principles (*asraya*) of those who proclaim theories of causality and does not admit the cause to have any efficiency with regard to the effect; but, since one sees various things such as seeds and the like which produce effects, therefore Nature is not the cause.

An agent which is single cannot at all be the cause of things which are manifold; therefore as Nature is described as single in essence, it is not the cause of mundane evolution (*pravrthi*).

Since Nature is asserted to be all-pervading, it follows that it can produce no effect; and, since one sees no form of result (of a cause) except effects, therefore Nature is not a cause of production.

Since it is all-pervading, it should, by reason of its being the cause, be the universal cause of everything unceasingly; but since we see a limitation in the activity (of a cause) to its (individual) result, therefore Nature is not a cause o f production.

Since it is established that it is without attribute *(guna)*, there should be no attribute in its results; but since we see everything in the world to have attributes, therefore Nature is not the cause of mundane evolution.

Since, as a perpetual cause, it can have no special characteristics *(visesa)*, there can never be any specific attribute in its evolutes *(vikara)*; and since specific attributes are found to be present in the evolutes, therefore there is no productivity from Nature.

Since Nature is productive in essence, no cause of destruction is established with respect to its results; and, since we observe the destruction of the evolutes, therefore we must hold the cause at work to be something different.

Since union subsists with that which has the potentiality (of causing rebirth), nothing is gained by ascetics *(yati)* desirous of absolute salvation *(sunaisthika moksa)*; for, since the continuance of activity is the essence of man's nature, how can they be released (from this life) except to pass on (to renewed activity) in the beyond ?

The action of Nature, they say, is not perceptible *(avyakta)* to the mind, yet it is said to have perceptible evolutes. Therefore Nature is not a cause of the continuance of activity; for it is established that a result in the world can only proceed from a cause which is equally manifest.

An inanimate *(acetana?)* Nature cannot have for its effects animate beings such as horses, oxen or mules; for nothing animate proceeds from inanimate causes.

Just as a garland of gold is a special form *(visesa)*, so

the evolutes of Nature are special forms; and, since the result is a special form, while the cause is not one, therefore Nature has no productive efficiency.

If Time is postulated as the creator of the world, then there is no liberation for seekers. For the cause of the world would be perpetually productive, so that men would have no end.

Some see the determining principle as the selfness in the matters *(dravya)*, which is one and is made manifold by the attributes *(guna)*; though they take their stand on a single cause, yet it has separate characteristics *(bhinnavisesa)*.

The attribute-theorist sees in the variety of attributes the operation of matter, which is born from a certain maturation *(paka?)*. Since the cause is held to be not different (from the effect), one must conclude that the matters are ineffective *(sunya)*.

Certainly the unmanifested *(avyakta)*, from which matter arises, cannot be the subject of a valid inference; for by perception *(piratyaksatah)* we do not see in fact the development of a result which is manifest from that which is unmanifest.

As for the result which first arises from the unmanifest and comes into activity from the pair of manifests, from it (sc. the unmanifest?) which is postulated arises in this world the great one *(mahat)* which is not postulated, and there ensue the defects of the Nature-hypothesis.

If Man *(purusa)* were the cause with respect to the effect, everyone would certainly obtain whatever he wanted; yet in this world some desires remain unfulfilled, and against their will *(avasa)* men get what they do not want.

If it were a matter within his own control, man would not let himself be born as an ox, horse, mule or camel; for since men perform the acts they want and hate suffering, who would bring suffering on himself ?

If Man were the agent in the world, he would certainly do what is agreeable to himself, not what is disagreeable; yet in the execution of his wishes the undesired is done as well as the desired, and who, if he were the controller of events *(mahesvara)*, would carry out the undesired ?

Whereas man is afraid of evil *(adharma)* and strives to attain the good *(dharma)*, yet the various sins carry him away against his will; therefore in this matter man falls into bondage to an outside force *(paratantra)*.

Man has no dominion over himself but is subject to others; for we see the effects of cold, heat, rain, thunderbolts and lightning to frustrate his efforts. Therefore Man is not master *(isvara)* over the effects.

Inasmuch as corn grows from the seed with the support of soil and water and by union with the right season, and as fire originates front the wood and blazes with the addition of ghee there is no absence of cause such as is called existence without a cause.

If the activity of the world proceeded without a cause, there would be no action by men. Everyone would obtain everything, and inevitably there would be universal (sarvatragamin?) accomplishment in this world.

Seeing that, if pleasure and suffering were without a cause, there would be no apportionment of pleasure and suffering to everyone, and pleasure and suffering would not be comprehensible without a cause, therefore this which is called "without a cause" is not a cause.

He knew that these and the like disparate causes do not cause the activity of the world. He saw the world not to be without a cause and he comprehended these defects of causelessness.

The various beings too, moving and stationary, come into existence in dependence on various causes; there is nothing in the world without a cause, yet the world does not know the universal cause.

Then *Sudatta*, having been given that good gift, understood the good Law of the Great Seer, Whose Law is noble, and with mind unalterably fixed in faith, addressed these words to Him;—

"My dwelling stands in Sravasti, a city renowned for

virtue and ruled by the scion of Haryasva's race. There I wish to make a monastery for You; deign to accept that flawless excellent abode.

Although, O Sage, I see that You are indifferent to whether You live in a palace or a lonely forest, yet, O Arhat, out of compassion for me You should accept it for a dwelling."

Then He knew that he intended to give and that his mind was liberated. So He, Whose mind was free from passion and Who knew the intentions, uttered His intention with the greatest gentleness (or, calm):—

"Your resolution is firm, (though you dwell) among treasures transitory as lightning, and your being is set *(adhimuc)* on giving. It is no wonder then that you should see the truth, rejoicing as you do by nature in the Law and delighting in giving.

Whatever goods are taken out of a burning house are not burnt up; similarly when the world is being burnt up with the fire of death *(kala)*, a man gains whatever he gives away.

Therefore the liberal-minded know giving to be the real *(samyak)* enjoyment of the objects of sense. But niggardly men, seeing the danger of exhaustion (of their wealth), do not give for fear they may have nothing to enjoy.

Giving wealth *(artha)* at the right time to a proper recipient *(patra)* is like fighting with heroism and pride. The man who is eminent in resolution knows this, but not others, and he alone gives and fights with determination.

Because he is a giver, who fares through the world delighting in giving and thereby obtains fame and a good name, good men honour him for his generosity and associate with him.

Thus he is at ease in the world and does not fall into sin from lack of longsuffering. Ever contented, because he claims to have done good, in the hour of death he is not affrighted.

The fruit of the gift in this world may be some flowers,

yet in the hereafter he will obtain the reward of the giver. For there is no friend like unto liberality for man who revolves on the wheel of the cycle of existence.

Those who are born in the world of men or in the heavens receive a station superior to their equals by reason of their charity; those too who are born as horses or elephants, will obtain the fruit by becoming chiefs (of horses or elephants).

By means of the gift he will go to heaven, surrounded by enjoyments and protected by his discipline. The man who is tranquillized and conducts himself with knowledge *(jnanapurvam) is* without support *(asraya)* and does not go the way of number.

He practises liberality also in order to obtain deathlessness and delights in thinking (*smr*) on giving; his mind by reason of that delight certainly becomes concentrated.

With this success *(samudaya)* in concentration of mind gradually he comes to a knowledge of birth and suppression; for by giving to others, the sins that abide in the heart of the giver of the gift are diminished.

First, it is said, the giver cuts off attachment to those goods which he gives away, and since he gives with an affectionate mind, he thereby abandons wrath and pride.

In the case of the giver who rejoices on seeing the recipients' pleasure and is therefore not niggardly, and who reflects on the fruit of the gift, scepticism *(nastitva}* and the darkness of ignorance are destroyed.

Therefore giving is one of the elements of salvation, since by it are subdued the avarice to which the ignoble resort and the thirst by which the habit of giving is destroyed; for when it is present, there is salvation by destruction of the sins.

Just as some like trees for their shade, some for their fruit and some for their flowers, so some employ themselves in giving for the sake of quietude, others for the sake of wealth.

Therefore in particular householders do not store up their goods, but give according to their means; and since it is giving which alone bestows value on wealth, this is the path for the good to follow.

The giver of food gives strength, the giver of clothes too beauty, but he who gives an abode for the religious gives everything in the world.

The giver of a vehicle also gives comfort, and the giver of a lamp illumination. Hence he who preaches the Law of ultimate beatitude gives the deathlessness that cannot be taken away.

Some give gifts for the sake of the passions, others for riches, others for fame, some for heaven, others in order not to be wretched *(krpana?)*; but this gift of yours has no ulterior motive.

Therefore bravo to you, who have formed such a desire; and when you have brought your intention to fulfilment, be contented. You, who came here possessed of passion *(rajas)* and the darkness of ignorance *(tamas)*, will go away with your mind purified by knowledge."

He who had come rightly to the real truth by the path, full of joy and..., took the matter of the Vihara much to heart and set off in due course with Upatisya.

Thereon he came to the capital of the Kosala king and wandered about in search of a site for the Vihara. Then he saw the garden of Jeta, majestic and suitable, with trees entrancing in their beauty.

Then in order to buy it he visited Jeta, who was too attached to it to sell it. "Even," he said, "if you were to cover it entirely with money, still I would not let you have the land."

Then Sudatta said to him there, "I have need (?) of the garden," and persisted in his desire for it. Then he covered it with treasure and, looking on it as a business *(vyavahara)* of the Law, he bought it.

When Jeta saw that he was giving the money, he became extremely devoted to the Buddha, and gave up to the Tathagata the rest of the grove in its entirety.

Then with Upatisya, the great seer, in charge of the works

as Superintendent, Anathapindada determined to do it quickly, and with mind liberated and unattached, he started to build a mighty Vihara, glorious in beauty.

And the embodiment of his wealth and power and insight, even like the palace of the Lord of Wealth come down to earth, and like the Fortune of the Northern Kosala capital, and like the stage *(bhumi)* of Tathagatahood.

19

FATHER AND SON

Then the Sage, having overcome by His knowledge all the teachers of the various systems, set forth in due course from the city of the Five Mountains for that inhabited by his royal father.

Then the thousand disciples He had just converted went too. He arrived at his father's realm, and then, in order to do him a favour, stayed near His native city.

Then the purohita and the wise minister, hearing the joyful news from their trustworthy spies that the Noble One had returned with His aim accomplished, respectfully informed the king.

Then the king, learning of His arrival, was filled with joy, and desiring to see Him, set out to meet Him with a cortege of all the citizens, forgetful in his haste of all decorum *(dhairya)*.

He saw Him in the distance surrounded by His disciples, like Brahma in the midst of the seers; and out of respect for the Law of the Great Seer, he alighted from his chariot and approached on foot.

Hastening into His presence, at the sight of the Sage he uttered no words; for he was as incapable of calling Him "Mendicant" as of calling Him "Son."

Then as he looked at His mendicant's robes and contemplated the various ornaments on his own person, his sighs came fast, and shedding tears he lamented in an undertone:—

"Like a traveller overcome by thirst, who approaches the distant pool to find it dried up, my affliction becomes overwhelming on seeing Him sitting close by me calmly and without change of feeling.

As I look on that same form of His, as one might look at the pictured representation of a dear one, still remembered in mind, but abiding at the end of the world, I feel no delight just as He feels none.

The earth, engirdled by all the mountains, should belong to Him, as it did to Mandhatr in the golden age; yet He, Who should not beg even from a king, now lives by begging from others.

He dwells here, surpassing Meru in steadfastness, the sun in brightness, the moon in beauty, a great elephant in stride, a bull in voice; yet He eats the food of mendicancy instead of winning the earth."

Then the Buddha knew that His father still thought of Him in his mind as his son, and in His compassion for the monarch *(lokadhideva)* He flew up into the sky for his sake.

He touched the chariot of the sun with His hand and walked on foot in the path frequented by the wind; He transformed His single body into many and then made the many bodies into one.

Without impediment He plunged into the earth as if into water, and walked on the surface of the water as if on dry land; and He calmly (*prasanna*?) penetrated the mountain, passing through it as free from obstruction as if moving through the air.

With one half of His body He emitted showers of rain, and with the other He blazed as if with fire. He appeared in the sky shining gloriously, as brilliant as the bright herbs on the mountain.

Thus He produced delight in the mind of the king, who was so fond of Him and, seated in the sky like a second sun, He expounded the Law to the ruler of men:—

"I know, O king, that in your compassionate nature you are overtaken by sorrow at the sight of Me. Give up that delight in having a son, and, becoming calm, accept from Me the Law in place of a son.

What no son has ever before given to a father, what

no father has ever before received from a son, that which is better than a kingdom or than Paradise, know that, O king, to be the most excellent deathlessness.

Guardian of the earth, recognize the nature of the act, the birthplace of the act, the vehicle *(asraya)* of the act and the lot that comes by maturation of the act, and know the world to be under the dominion of the act; therefore practise that act which is advantageous.

Consider and ponder on the real truth of the world. The good act is man's friend, the bad one the reverse. You must abandon everything (when you die) and go forth alone, without support *(asraya)*, accompanied only by your acts.

The world of the living fares on under the impulse *(asraya)* of the act, whether in heaven or hell, among animals or in the world of men. The cause of existence is threefold, threefold the birthplace *(yoni)*, and various are the deeds that men commit.

Therefore rightly direct yourself to the other alternative (or, the class of two, *dvivarga)* and purify the actions of your body and voice. Strive for quietude of the mind. This is your goal; there is no other.

Knowing' the world to be restless as the waves of the sea and meditating on it, you should take no joy in the spheres of existence, and should practise that act which is virtuous and leads to the highest good, in order to destroy the power of the act.

Know that the world ever revolves like the circle of the asterisms; even the gods pass their peak and fall from heaven, how much less then may one rely on the human state ?

Know the bliss of salvation to be the supreme bliss, and internal *(adhyatma)* delight to be the highest of all delights. What self-controlled *(atmavat)* man rejoices in the pleasures of splendour, seeing that it is attended by many dangers, like a house infested with snakes ?

Look therefore on the world as encompassed with great dangers like a house on fire, and seek for that stage which is tranquil and certain, and in which there is neither birth nor death, neither toil nor suffering.

Crush the hostile armies of the faults, for which there is no need of wealth or territory or weapons or horses or elephants. Once they are conquered, there is nothing more to conquer.

Comprehend suffering, the cause of suffering, the appeasement and the means of appeasement. By thoroughly penetrating these four, the great danger and the evil births *(durgati)* are suppressed."

Then, since the Blessed One's display of miraculous power had previously made the king's mind a fit field for instruction, now on receiving His Law by hearing, he was thrilled and folding his hands he uttered these words:—

"Wise and fruitful are Your deeds, in that You have released me from great suffering. I, who formerly rejoiced in the calamitous gift of the earth for the increase of grief, now rejoice in the fruit of having a son.

Rightly *(sthane)* You went away, abandoning sovereign glory. Rightly You toiled with great labour, and rightly, beloved as You were, Yon left Your dear relations and have had compassion on us.

For the good of the distressed world You have also obtained this final beautitude, which not even the divine seers or the royal seers arrived at in olden times.

If You had become a universal monarch *(cakravartin),* You would not have caused me such joy as I now firmly feel by the sight of these magic powers and of Your Law.

If You had remained bound up with life here even in this existence, You would as a Cakravartin have protected mankind, but now as a Sage, having broken down the great suffering of the cycle of existence, You preach the Law for the sake of the world.

By displaying these miraculous powers and deep-searching wisdom and by completely overcoming the perils of the cycle of existence, even without sovereignty You have become the Lord (*isvara*) in the world, but even with sovereignty prospering You would not have become so, it helplessly conjoined with existence."

Many such things spoke the Sakya king, who had become fit (to receive) the teaching of the Compassionate One's Law, and, though he stood in the position of king and father, yet he did obeisance to his Son, because he had penetrated the truth.

Many persons, who had witnessed the Sage's possession of miraculous power, who had understood the doctrine *(sastra)* that pierced through to the real truth, and who saw the king His father reverencing Him, conceived a desire to leave their homes.

Then many princes, in possession of the fruit of their deeds, adopted that method of religion *(dharmavidhi),* and, regardless of the Vedic Scriptures *(mantra)* and their great means of enjoyment, abandoned their loving weeping families.

Ananda, Nanda, Krmila, Aniruddha, Nanda, Upananda, and also Kunthadhana, and Devadatta, the false teacher of the disciples, after instruction by the Sage, left their homes.

Then the purohita's son, the great-souled Udayin, went forth on the same path; and Upali, the son of Atri (or, the Atreya), seeing their decision, made up his mind to the same course.

The king too, seeing his Son's power, entered the stream of the supreme deathlessness, and dead to attachment he handed over the realm to his brother and abode in the palace, behaving as a royal seer.

The Buddha, having converted these and other relations, friends and followers, entered the city at the proper time in full control of Himself amid the welcome of the weeping citizens.

Hearing the news that the King's Son, Sarvarthasiddha, His task accomplished, was entering the town, the women in the palaces rushed to the doors and windows.

When the women saw Him clad in the ochre-coloured robe, yet shining like the sun half-covered by an evening cloud, they shed tears and, folding their lotus-like hands, did obeisance to Him.

As the women saw Him proceeding with down-gazing face, illuminated by the Law and the beauty of His person, they manifested pity and devotion, and, their eyes turbid with tears, they thus lamented:—

"His beautiful body is transformed by the shaving of His head and the wearing of cast off garments, yet He is enveloped in the colour of gold from His body. So He walks, directing His eyes on the ground.

He Who was worthy to shelter under the white umbrella, to . ., to . . . and to be a conqueror, now goes along, holding the begging-bowl.

He Who ought to ride on a horse under the shelter of an umbrella, white as the face of a beautiful woman, when a *tamala* leaf has been applied to her cheek, goes on foot, holding the begging-bowl.

He Who should be humbling enemy princes and Who, wearing a brilliant headdress, should be gazed at by troops of women and by His attendant retinue, walks along looking at only a yoke's length of ground in front of Him.

What is this system *(darsana)* of His, what these mendicant's badges, what goal does He seek, why has pleasure become His enemy, that He should delight in vows, not in children and wives ?

The king's daughter-in-law, Yasodhara, was certainly gripped by grief, yet what a difficult thing she did, that, on hearing of this her Lord's conduct, she survived the news and did not pass to destruction.

When too the lord of men sees his Son's form shining in accordance with His beauty but no longer adorned *(vivarna)*, does he remain, fond of his Son, or does he look on Him as a harmful enemy ?

If, on seeing His son Bahula bathed in tears, He feels no attachment to him, what is one to think o£ such resolute vows that turn a man's face away from his affectionate kinsfolk ?

Neither His lustre, nor the form of His body, nor His stride have been destroyed by the practice of pleasure; and yet, shining with these qualities, He has come to quietude and separated Himself from the objects of sense."

Thus the women uttered many laments, grasping at different opinions like the various teachers. The Buddha too with His mind untouched entered His native city and, obtaining alms, returned to the Nyagrodha grove.

With mind free from desire the Tathagata had entered His father's town for alms; and He kept in mind His wishes to liberate the folk, whose means were small from their not having practised good (in the past) and who could give but little alms, to strengthen the brethren *(sramana)*, who had not gained control of their minds and who did not find contentment by such proceedings (i.e. alms-seeking), to be able to answer "Happiness be yours "(?) to the world, and similarly to preach the Scriptures (?).

20

JETAVANA

(The Buddha), having had compassion on the great multitude (in Kapilavastu), set forth with a mighty following for the city guarded by the arm of Prasenajit.

Then he arrived at the glorious Jetavana, brilliant with the outspread bloom of its *asoka* trees, resonant with the voices of intoxicated cuckoos, and having a row of lofty dwellings, white as the snow of Kailasa.

Then taking an ewer of pure water, which was embossed with gold and adorned with a white wreath, Sudatta in due course presented the Jetavana to the Tathagata.

Then king Prasenajit, desiring to see the Sage of the Sakyas, set off for the Jetavana. Then on his arrival he reverently did Him obeisance, and sitting down thus addressed Him:—

"Your desire, O Sage, to stay in this city will certainly bring good fortune to the Kosala people. For is not the country, which has not the support of such a Knower of the real truth *(tattvadarsin),* ruined or unfortunate?

Or rather at the sight of You and at Your acceptance of our obeisance in order to do us a favour, a satisfaction is now ours, such as is not felt by men even on meeting with the good.

The wind assumes the nature (i.e. scent) of whatever thing it blows upon; and birds, by gaining contact with Meru, lose their natural selves and are turned to gold.

Therefore it is only by obtaining the residence in it of a saintly Being, Who is Lord of this world and of the hereafter, that my grove is glorious to see, like the palace of Trisanku, when it received the great sage, the son of Gadhin (Visvamitra).

The various gains that are won in the world are transitory and come to an end, but for those countless things which arise from proximity to You there is no destruction.

O Saint *(sadhu)*, no gain is known outside this, namely the sight of Your doctrine (?). O Lord, I have suffered and been harassed by passion *(raga)* and the kingly profession *(raja-dharma)*."

The Sage listened graciously to these and other such words from the Indra-like king, and knowing him to be addicted to rapacity and lust, replied thus to stir up his mind:—

"O king, it is no great wonder that you should speak thus or act thus towards the saintly . . .

Those who desire to come up from below ... to the righteous people who desire their benefit ...

Since, O guardian of the earth, such is your state of mind. I desire therefore to say somewhat to you. Do you then comprehend My teaching and so act that it may be fruitful.

Lord of men, when Time binds and drags away the king. neither relations nor friends nor sovereignty will follow you; all will depart, afflicted and helpless. Your deeds alone will accompany you like a shadow.

Therefore guard your kingdom according to the Law, if you desire Paradise and a good reputation. For there is no kingdom at all in Paradise for the king who in his delusion misapplies *(akulaya?)* the Law.

By guarding his kingdom in this world according to the Law Krsasva gained Heaven, while the lord of men, Nikumbha, resiling from the Law in this world out of delusion, entered the earth in Kasi.

I have given you this example, My friend *(saumya)*, of good *(arya)* and evil deeds. Therefore ever guard your subjects well, and with due reflection strive steadfastly for the right.

Thus do not harass human beings, never give free play to your senses; do not consort with the vicious or give way to anger, do not let your mind wander on evil courses.

Do not trouble *(muh?)* virtuous people through pride, do not oppress *(han)* ascetics who are to be treated as friends *(mitrasamjna)*, do not undertake holy vows under the influence of sin, and do not adhere at all to evil views.

Do not resort to the marvellous (?), be not addicted to evil deeds, be not affected by arrogance *(mada)*, do not listen with displeasure or intolerance, do not exhaust (?) your fame or fix your mind on falsehood, do not take land revenue in excess of the share allowed by the laws *(sastra)*.

Keep your mind level and carry out the Law, consort with the good and. ..; so act that, having obtained this eminence (as king now), you may arrive again (in the next life) at a noble position.

Applying energy *(virya)*, grasping steadfastness *(dhairya)*. producing learning *(vidyah)*, overcoming the sins *(dosa)*, do the work of a religious man (arya) in constant recollection of death, and winning a great position gain possession of the path.

You should, my friend, again do that work which protects this fruit; for the prudent man, who has done this deed (in the past), sows the seed whose fruit he has seen.

In this world he who, being in a lofty position, gives way to sin, is in the light, but his mind stands in darkness; but he who is devoted *(pradhana)* to the Law yet is not a chief among men, is in darkness, but his mind stands in the light.

Whoever, being of high degree, practises the way of the Law, his mind becomes extremely white (*sukla?*); and whoever, being of low degree, does sinful acts, his mind becomes extremely dark.

Therefore, O king, knowing the existence of these four groups, exert yourself as you will; but if you wish to fare in pleasure, you will find yourself in the three lower classes, not in the first.

It is impossible for a man to do good *(kusala)* for another's account, or, if he does it, it does not accrue to the other. The effect of one's own act is not destroyed, but is experienced by oneself, and the accrual of what is not done is not accepted as a fact.

Since what is not done has no efficacy, that which is not done does not turn to good *(sreyas)* in the hereafter, and, as thereby there is not even cessation of existence *(vibhava)* in the world, therefore exert yourself in the method of good deeds.

The wicked man who commits sin to excess has no enjoyment in himself in the world of the living. Having committed his own sins to his own account, in the hereafter he will certainly experience the fruit himself.

Four great mountains, O mighty king, come together and crush the world; what is there to be done except with the support *(asraya)* of the various deeds done in accordance with the Law to the best of one's capacity *(yathopapattau)?*

Similarly when these four, birth,' old age, disease and eke death come together, the entire world revolves helplessly, encompassed as it were by four mountains.

When then this suffering comes on us against our will, and against it we have neither support nor power of resistance nor protection, there is no resource *(ausadhi?)* for us to take except the Law, which is unfailing and inexhaustible.

Therefore, inasmuch as the world is impermanent and given to sensual pleasures, which are transitory as a flash of lightning, and as it stands on the fingertips of Death, man should not undergo the fruit of not following the Law.

Those various king's, who were like Great Indra, fought even in the divine battles and were mighty and proud (?), yet in course of time suffering was their lot.

Even the earth that supports all beings is destroyed, and Meru is burnt up by the cosmic fire; the mighty ocean dries up, how much more then does the world of man, transitory as foam, go to destruction ?

The wind blows violently and yet dies down, the sun scorches the world and yet goes to its setting, the fire too blazes and yet becomes extinguished; all that is, I ween, is in such case and subject to change.

This body, though long guarded with care and cherished with various enjoyments, yet abiding here but a few days . . .

Know that in this state of the world men, fostering pride and arrogance *(mada),* in time lie down to sleep on lofty couches; do not lie down on them, but keep awake for the sake of the highest good.

The world mounts the ever-moving swing of the cycle of existence, and is heedless, though its fall is certain . . .

Do not resort to that which does not have pleasant consequences *(sambandha?),* do not do that which has evil fruit; he is not a friend who is not conjoined with good, that is not knowledge which does hot dispel suffering.

If you have knowledge, there is no more existence for you, or if there is existence, it is in the bodiless state; for, it you continue incarnated in a body, you are not released from the objects of sense, and the sphere of passion is ephemeral and calamitous.

Since even the Arupa deities, as still subject to the power of the act, are impermanent and under the dominion of Time, therefore set your mind on the cessation of activity *(apravrtti);* if there is no activity, there is no suffering.

Since the body is the root of suffering in view of its dependence on the various actions such as moving, standing and the like, therefore the debt of the body is acquitted by the existence of knowledge which is competent with regard to the bodiless state.

Since the world comes to birth by reason of passion and thereby undergoes much great suffering, therefore when a man can detach himself *(vivic)* from the sphere of passion *(kamabhava),* he is no longer attached to suffering and ceases to be afflicted.

Therefore whether among the Rupa deities or among the Rupa deities who are still subject to the lusts *(kama),* the continuance of activity is not stilled because of the liability to transmigration, how much more then is it not so for those in the domain *(pracara)* of the six lusts ?

Seeing the three spheres of existence to be thus impermanent, suffering and without self, and to be ever on fire, there is no place of refuge for men to enter, as for birds whose roosting-tree is ablaze.

This is the best thing to be known, nothing else is to be known. This is the best wisdom *(mati)*, nothing else is wisdom. This is the best task, nothing else is admitted (to be such)...

It is certainly not to be thought that this Law is not for those who dwell in houses. Whether abiding in the forest or in the house, only he really exists who achieves quietude.

A man, when scorched with heat, enters the water, and everyone obtains relief from a cloud. He who has a lamp sees in the darkness. Yoga is the means *(pramana)*, not age nor family.

Some, though they live in the forest in their old age *(vayas)*, fail to practise yoga, and, breaking their vows, descend to an evil existence *(durgati)*; others, though living in their homes, purify their actions and, taking proper heed, attain to the final beatitude.

Among the folk struggling in the ocean of ignorance *(tamas)*, whose waves are wrong views and whose water existence, only he who has the boat of mystic wisdom *(prajna)* with the oars of awareness and energy is rescued therefrom."

Thus the king, who was much given to the objects of sense, received this truth *(tattva)* of the Law from the Omniscient and, with the conviction born in him that evil kingship is impermanent and unstable, returned to Sravasti in sober mood like an elephant freed from must.

The other doctors of learning *(tirthika)*, knowing that the lord of the earth had bowed down to Him, challenged Him of the Ten Forces to a display of magic powers; and, when the guardian of the earth requested Him to do so, the Seer Who had conquered self consented to exhibit His magic might.

Then the Sage shone with an orb diffusing splendour, like the rising sun outshining the stars, and He defeated the teachers of the various systems by magic powers of many kinds, giving general delight (?).

Then after the people of Sravasti had honoured and reverenced Him therefor, He departed with the extremes ! *(niruttara?)* majesty and mounted above the triple universe in order to preach the Law for the benefit of His mother.

Then the Sage converted by His knowledge His mother who dwelt in Heaven; and passing the rainy season there and accepting alms in due form from the ruler of the Sky-gods, He descended from the heavenly worlds to Samkasya.

The gods, who had acquired tranquillity, stood in their mansions and followed Him with their eyes, as if they were falling to earth, and the various kings on earth, raising their faces to the sky, received Him with their heads, as they did obeisance to Him.

21

THE MISSION

After converting in Heaven His mother and the heavenly dwellers who were desirous of salvation, the Sage travelled over the earth, converting those who were due for conversion by Him.

Then in the city that lies in the midst of the five mountains, the Teacher *(Vinayaka)* converted Jyotiska, Jivaka, Sura, Srona and Angada.

He turned from their former views the king's son, Abhaya, Srigupta, Upali, Nyagrodha and others, who held the (views of the two) ends (permanence and annihilation).

He converted the lord of Gandhara, Puskara by name, who abandoned his royal glory immediately on hearing the Law.

Then He, Whose energy *(parakrama)* was extensive *(vipula),* converted on Mount Vipula the Yaksas Haimavata and Satagra.

The Knower of qualities (*gunadarsin*) brought to the faith at night in Jivaka's mango-grove the king (Ajatasatru) accompanied by his five hundred queens.

Then on Mount Pasana the Brahman Parayana, who was intent on quietude, started the study of the meanings decided by subtle words.

Then in Venukantaka He converted the saintly mother of Nanda, who by good awareness (*satsmrti*) saw (hidden) treasures before her eyes.

Then in the village of Sthanumati the excellent Brahman Kutadatta, who wished to sacrifice with all sorts of sacrifices, was caused to enter the Law of Salvation.

Then on the Videha mountain Pancasikha and the Asuris (?) and gods entered into firm conviction.

Then in the city of Anga the Yaksa Purnabhadra and the great snakes, Srestha, Danda, Sveta (?) Pingala (?) and Canda (?) were converted.

In the city of Apana the Brahmans Kenya and Sela, who were practicing austerities (for the sake of being reborn in heaven), were brought to salvation.

Among the Suhmas the Holy One by the night of His magic power converted Angulimala, a Brahman who was cruel like Saudasa.

In Bhadra the son of a gentleman *(bhadra)*, Mendhaka by name, of good livelihood and a generous giver, and like Purnabhadra in wealth, was caused to take the right views.

Then in the city of Videha the Best of speakers overcame by His preaching him who was named Brahmayus, and whose lifetime was as extensive as Brahma's.

He converted the flesh-eating monster (Markata) in the pool at Vaisali as well as the Licchavis headed by Simha, and Uttara(?) and Satyaka.

Then in the city of Alakavati He, Whose work was good, brought to the way of the Law the Yaksa Bhadra, who possessed a good disposition.

Then in a very evil forest *(atavi)* the Wise One instructed the Yaksa Atavika and the young prince *(kumara)* Hastaka.

Then in the city of . . . He Who saw salvation preached salvation to the Yaksa Nagayana(?), while the Yaksa king did obeisance.

At Gaya the Seer instructed the Tamkita(?) sages and the two Yaksas, Khara and Suciloma.

Then in the town of Varanasi the Possessor of the Ten Forces converted the Brahman Katyayana, nephew of Asita the sage.

Then He went by His magic powers to the city of Surparaka and in due course instructed the merchant Stavakarnin,

Who, on being instructed, became so faithful that he started to build for the Best of seers a sandalwood Vihara, which was ever odorous and touched the sky.

Then He converted Kapila the ascetic in Mahivati, where the wheel-marks of the Sage's feet were seen on a stone.

Then in Varana He instructed the Yaksa Varana; similarly in Mathura the fierce Gardabha was converted.

Then in the town of Sthulakosthaka the Teacher converted him who was called Rastrapala, whose wealth was equal to that of a king.

Then in Vairanja a great being (or, crowd) like Virnica was converted, and similarly in Kalmasadamya the learned Bharadvaja (?).

In Sravasti again the Sage dispelled the darkness of Sabhiya, of the Nirgrantha Naptriputras and of the other doctors (*tirthika*).

Here too the Brahman sacrificers *(yajnaka),* Puskalasadin(?) and Jatisroni(?), as well as the king of Kosala, were brought to believe on the Buddha.

Then in the forest land of Setavika the Best of teachers taught a parrot and a starling *(sarika),* birds *(dvija)* who were as learned as Brahmans.

Then in the town of ... the savage Nagara (?) and Kalaka and Kumbhira whose deeds were ferocious were brought to tranquillity.

Then among the Bhargasas (Bhargas?) He converted, the Yaksa Bhesaka and favoured, similarly the aged parents of Nakula. In Kausambi the wealthy Ghosila, Kubjottara and other women, and a multitude beside were converted.

Then in the Gandhara country the snake Apalala, with his senses tamed by the Rule, passed, beyond evil.

Then the Wise One in due course preached sermons, after converting . . ., who desired to burn up like Death.

By the conversion of these and other beings, whether faring on earth or in the sky, the fame of the Buddha kept on waxing like the ocean at springtide *(parvani).*

Devadatta, seeing His greatness *(mahatmya),* became envious and, losing control over the trances, he did many improper things.

With his mind sullied he created a schism in the Sage's community, and by reason of the separation, instead of being devoted to Him, he endeavoured to do Him hurt.

Then he set a rock rolling with force on Mount Grdhrakuta; but, though aimed at the Sage, it did not fall on Him but divided into two pieces.

On the royal highway he set loose in the direction of the Tathagata a lord of elephants, whose trumpeting was as the thundering of the black clouds at the dissolution of the world, and whose rushing as the wind in the sky when the moon is obscured.

The streets of Rajagrha became impassable through the corpses, which he had struck with his body or taken up with his trunk or whose entrails were drawn out by his tusks and scattered in heaps.

In his thirst for flesh he dug into men's thighs, and when his trunk touched the entrails, he cast twitching wreaths of them, as though they were stones, into the air to free himself while his fearsome head, ears and tongue dripped with blood.

The townsfolk were panicstruck and terrified of him, as he wandered in limitless fury, stained with drops of gore and putrescent blood, and imbued with the smell of the ichor that spread over his forehead.

As they saw the maddened elephant, like the fearsome club of Death (Yama), with his face swollen with insolence, trumpeting and rolling his eyes in wrath, cries of "Woe! Woe!" arose from Rajagrha.

Some ran despairingly in all directions, some hid in places where they could not be seen, and others, so frightened as to be afraid of nothing else, entered the houses of others.

Some took no account of their lives in their tear that the elephant might hurt the Buddha, and valiantly shouted behind him, uttering roars like a lion about to spring.

Similarly others called out to the mahout; some raised their hands to him imploringly, some too threatened him then, and others appealed to his love of money.

The young women, looking on from the balconies, flung their arms about and wept; some in terror covered their eyes with copper-coloured hands, which had golden bracelets.

Despite the on-coming (?) elephant intent on slaughter,

despite the weeping people holding up their arms (in warning), the Blessed One advanced, collected and unmoved, not breaking His step nor giving way to malevolence.

Quietly the Sage came on; for not even that great lord of elephants had power to touch Him, since in His benevolence *(maitri)* He had compassion on all creatures and since the gods followed Him from devotion.

The disciples who were following the Buddha fled, on seeing the great elephant from afar. Ananda alone followed the Buddha, just as the inherent nature follows the multiform world.

Then, as the enraged elephant drew near, he came to his senses through the Sage's spiritual power *(prabhava)*, and, letting his body down, he placed his head on the ground, like a mountain whose wings have been shattered by a thunderbolt.

Just as the sun touches a cloud with its rays, the Sage stroked the lord of elephants on the head with His beautiful hand, soft as a lotus and having well-formed webbed fingers.

As the elephant bent low at His feet, like a black raincloud overladen with water, the Sage, seeing his palmleaf-like ears to be moveless, preached to him the religious peace, which is fit for rational beings:—

"The slaughter of the Sinless One *(naga)* is accompanied by suffering; do no harm, O elephant, to the Sinless One. For, O elephant, the life of him who slays the Sinless does not develop from existence to existence in the eight good births.

The three, love, hatred and delusion, are intoxicants hard to conquer; yet the sages are free of the three intoxicants. Free yourself therefore of these fevers arid pass beyond sorrow.

Therefore in order to abandon this love of darkness, be quit of intoxication and resume your natural self. Do not, O lord of elephants, slip back through excess of passion into the mud of the ocean of transmigration."

Then the elephant, hearing these words, was freed from intoxication and returned to right feeling; and he obtained the good internal *(antargata)* pleasure, like one released from illness on drinking the elixir (amrta).

On seeing the lord of elephants straightway giying up his intoxication and doing obeisance as a pupil to the Sage, some flung up arms covered with clothes, others brandishing their arms let the clothes go.

Then some folded hands to the Sage, and others surrounded Him. Some praised the great elephant for his nobility *(aryatva),* and others, filled with wonder, stroked him.

Of the women in the palaces, some did Him honour with new clothes of great price, and others showered down on Him their various ornaments and fresh garlands of entrancing quality.

When that elephant, who was like Death *(kala),* stood humbled, those who did not believe entered the middle state, those who were already in the middle state reached a special degree of faith, and the believers were mightily strengthened.

Then Ajatasatru, standing in his palace, saw the lord of elephants tamed by the Sage and was overcome with amazement; joy grew in him, and he believed in the Buddha to the highest degree.

Just as, when the evil age passes away and the age of ascent begins, Law and Wealth increase, in such wise waxed the Sage by His fame, His magic powers, and His difficult undertakings.

But Devadatta, having in his malice done many evil and sinful deeds, fell to the regions below, execrated by king and people, by Brahmans and sages.

22

AT AMRAPALI GROVE

Then in course of time, when the Best of speakers had favoured the world and filled the earth with His Law, His mind turned to Nirvana.

Then in due time the Saint proceeded from Rajagrha to Pataliputra, where he stayed in the caitya known by the name of Patali.

Now at that time Varsakara, the minister of the Magadha king, had made a citadel to keep the Licchavis quiet.

The Tathagata saw the gods bringing their treasures there and prophesied that the city would become pre-eminent in the world.

The best of Doers, after being honoured in due form by Varsakara, proceeded with his disciples towards the chief wife of Ocean.

Then he (Varsakara) caused the gate, by which the Holy One, brilliant as the sun, emerged, to be reverenced as the Gautama Gate.

He, Who had seen the crossing (of the ocean of transmigration), came to the bank of the Ganges, and, seeing the people with their various boats available, reflected within Himself:—

"As it would be improper for Me to cross the river by effort, therefore I should go Myself without a boat by the force of My magic powers."

Thus unseen by the spectators, He with His disciples then passed to the other side in a moment, exceeding even the pace of the wind.

Inasmuch as the Sage knew that it is the boat of knowledge which crosses the ocean of suffering, He crossed the Ganges without again using this (i.e. a material?) boat.

The bank, from which the Teacher crossed to the other side of the Ganges, is famous in the world as a place of pilgrimage, known by His family name (Gautama).

Then the faces of the men, who wished to cross, who were crossing and who had crossed, opened wide in wonder, as their eyes fell on Him.

Then from the bank of the Ganges the Buddha went on to the village of Kuti, and, after preaching the Law there, went on to Nadlka.

Many people had died there at that time, and the Sage explained in what world each of them had been reborn and as what.

After passing one night there, the Srighana moved on to the city of Vaisali and abode in a glorious grove in the domain of Amrapali.

The courtesan Amrapali, hearing the Teacher was there, mounted a modest equipage and went forth with great joy.

She wore diaphanous white garments and was without garlands or body-paint, like a woman of good family at the time of worshipping the gods.

In the pride of her beauty, she attracted by her united charms the minds and the wealth of the Licchavi nobles.

Self-assured in her loveliness and glory, like a forest goddess in beauty, she descended from her chariot and quickly entered the grove.

The Blessed One, seeing that her eyes were flashing and that she was a cause of grief to women of family, commanded His disciples with voice like a drum:—

"This is Amrapali approaching, the mental fever of those whose strength is little; do you take your stand on knowledge, controlling your minds with the elixir of awareness.

Better is the neighbourhood of a snake or of an enemy with drawn sword, than that of woman for the man who is devoid of awareness and wisdom.

Whether sitting or lying down, whether walking or standing, or even when portrayed in a picture, woman carries away men's hearts.

Even if they be afflicted by disaster *(vyasana), or* fling their arms about weeping, or be burnt with dishevelled hair, yet women are pre-eminent in power.

Making use of extraneous things, they deceive by many adventitious *(aharya)* qualities, and concealing their real qualities they delude fools.

By seeing woman as impermanent, suffering, without self and impure, the minds of the adepts are not overcome on looking at her.

With minds well accustomed to these temptations *(alaya),* like cattle to their pastures, how can men be deluded when attacked by the pleasures of the gods?

Therefore taking the arrows of mystic wisdom, grasping the bow of energy in your hands and girding on the armour of awareness, think well on the idea of the objects of sense.

It is better to sear the eyes with red-hot iron pins than to look on woman's rolling eyes with misdirected awareness.

If at the moment of death your mind be subject to passion, it binds you helplessly and takes you to a rebirth among animals or in Hell.

Therefore recognize this danger and do not dwell on the external characteristics *(nimitta);* for he sees truly, who sees in the body only Matter *(rupa).*

In the world it is not the sense-organs which bind the objects, nor is it the objects which bind the senses. Whoever feels passion for them (the objects of sense), to them is he bound.

The objects and the sense organs are mutually attached, like two oxen harnessed to the same yoke.

The eye grasps the form and the mind considers it, and from that consideration arise passion with regard to the object and also freedom from passion.

If then great calamity ensues by not properly examining the objects of sense, activity in the domain of the senses is conjoined with all disasters.

Therefore not abandoning awareness, faring with the highest heedfulness, and having regard to your own good *(svartha)*, you should meditate *(bhavaya)* energetically with your minds."

While He thus instructed the disciples who had not proceeded to the end of the matter, Amrapali, seeing Him, drew near with folded hands.

Seeing the Seer seated with tranquil mind under a tree, she deemed herself highly favoured by His occupation *(paribhoga)* of the grove.

Then with great reverence, setting her eyes, restless as they were, in order, she did obeisance to the Sage with her head, which was like a *campaka* flower fully opened.

Then when she had seated herself in accordance with the Omniscient's directions, the Sage addressed her with words suited to her understanding:—

"This your intention is virtuous and your mind is steadfast by purification; yet desire for the Law is hard to find in a woman who is young and in the bloom of her beauty.

What cause'is there for wonder that the Law should attract men of intelligence *(dhimat?)* or women who are afflicted by misfortune *(vyasana)* or are self-controlled *(atmavat)* or ill?

But it is extraordinary that in the world solely devoted; *(ekaprasa)* to the objects of sense a young woman, by nature weak is comprehension and unsteady in mind, should entertain the idea of the Law.

Your mind is turned to the Law, that is your real wealth (*artha*); for since the world of the living is transitory, there are no riches outside the Law.

Health is borne down by illness, youth cut short by age, and life snatched away by death, but for the Law there is no such calamity *(vipat)*.

Since in seeking (for pleasure) one obtains only separation from the pleasant and association with the unpleasant, therefore the Law is the best path.

Dependence on others is great suffering, self-dependence the highest bliss; yet, when born in the race of Manu, all females are dependent on others.

Therefore you should come to a proper conclusion, since the suffering of women is excessive by reason equally of their dependence on others and of child-birth."

Young in years, but not like the young in disposition, intelligence and gravity, she listened joyfully to these words of the Great Sage.

Through the Tathagata's preaching of the Law, she cast aside the condition of mind that was given up to the lusts, and, despising the state of being a woman and turning aside from the objects of sense, she felt loathing for her means of livelihood.

Then entirely prostrating her slender body, like a mango-branch laden with blossom, she fixed her eye with devotion on the Great Sage and again stood with purified sight for the Law.

The woman, though modest by nature, yet ever spurred on by longing for the Law, joined her hands like a clump of lotuses *(pankajakara)* and spoke with gently uttered voice:—

"O Holy One, You have attained the goal and soothe suffering in the world. Deign in company with Your disciples to make the time of alms-seeking fruitful for me who am ripe for the fruit (?, *phalabhuta)*, in order that I may receive a sermon."

Then the Blessed One, seeing her to be so devoted, and knowing animate beings to be dependent on food, gave His consent by silence and announced His intention to her with a gesture *(vikara)*.

He, Who possessed the supreme Law and an eye that discerned occasions *(ksanakrtyarat?)*, rejoiced exceedingly in the vessel of the Law, knowing that the best gain is by faith, He praised her.

23

LIFE OF THE BODY

Then, understanding the Sage's intention, she did obeisance and returned to the town. The Licchavis, hearing the news, came to see the Buddha.

Some had white horses, chariots, umbrellas, garlands, ornaments and clothes; others again had them ruddy gold in hue.

Some had everything of beryl-yellow, and others of the colour of peacocks' tails. Thus gloriously apparelled, each to please himself, they came out.

With bodies vast as mountains and arms like golden yokes, they appeared like the glorious... in bodily form in heaven.

As they stood, about to alight from their chariots, they shone like streaks of lightning across an evening cloud *(samdhyabhrapada)*.

Inclining their waving headdresses, they gravely saluted the Sage; though full of pride, yet they stood there as if become sober in their desire for the Law.

Their passion-free *(rajohina?)* circle shone beside the Buddha like the bow of Indra (?) opposite the cloudless sun.

Then Simha and the others seated themselves on lion-seats decorated with gold, having the form *(samsthana?)* of lions on the ground, and the Man-lion said to them then:

"This devotion of yours to the Law far exceeds in value your distinctions such as beauty of form, sovereignty and strength.

Neither your beauty, nor your magnificent clothes, nor your ornaments or garlands, have the same brilliance as the virtues of discipline and the like have.

I hold the Vrjjis to be favoured and fortunate in that they have for lords you who are knowers of the Law and seekers of the Rule *(vinayaisin).*

O nobles *(arya),* protectors who abide in the Law are hard to find in due course for countries not outside the pale (of Aryavarta) and are not to be found for the unfortunate.

This country is favoured even by the Law, in that it is guarded by majestic nobles *(mahabhaga),* who protect the knowledge of the Law.

Therefore, just as cattle who want to cross a stream follow the herd-bull, so people flock to the country which is held by kings.

This discipline .should be ever present in yon, so that your riches *(svartha* ?) in this world and the next cannot be snatched away by the passions.

Great is the reward of discipline,—a contented mind, honour, gain renown, trust and delight, and in the hereafter bliss.

As the earth is the support of all beings, moving-and stationary, so discipline is the best support of all the virtues.

Know the man who abandons discipline and yet desires final beatitude to be like one without wings who wishes to fly, or like one without a boat who wishes to cross a river.

The man who, having renown and beauty and wealth, resiles from the discipline, resembles a tree loaded with flowers and fruit, yet covered with thorns.

A man may live in a palace and wear gorgeous clothes and ornaments, but, if he have discipline, his way of life is equal to that of a seer.

All are to be known as shams, who, though they wear dyed or bark garments and dress their hair in the various 'ascetic styles, have ruined their discipline.

Though he bathe three times a day at a sacred spot *(tirtha),* though he pour oblations twice in the fire, though he be scorched with fiery heat, if he have not discipline, he is nothing.

Though he deliver his body to beasts of prey, though he cast himself down a mountain, though he leap into fire or water, if he have not discipline, he is nothing.

Though lie subsist on a modicum of fruit and roots, though he graze the grass like a deer, though he desire to live on air, if he have not discipline, he is not cleansed.

The man, whose discipline is vile, is like the birds and beasts; he is not a vessel of the Law, but like a leaky vessel of water.

In the present life he reaps fear, ill report, mistrust and discontent, and in the hereafter he will incur (lit., eat) calamity.

Therefore discipline, like the guide in the desert, should not be killed; discipline, which is self-dependent and hard to acquire, is the boat that conveys man to Heaven.

Be whose mind is overcome by the sins loses everything in life. Taking your stand on discipline, destroy the sins and cherish faith.

Therefore he who desires progress *(bubhusu?)* should first rid himself of the thought of self; for the thought of self obscures the virtues, as smoke obscures the fire.

The virtues, even when really existent, do not shine, if overcome by pride, like the stars, sun and moon when covered by a great mass of cloud.

Arrogance *(auddhatya?)* destroys self-respect (*hri*), grief steadfastness, and old age beauty, and the thought of self destroys the roots of the virtues.

Because of envy and pride the Asuras, being defeated by the gods, were cast down to Patala, and Tripura was destroyed.

That man is not held to be wise, who in ephemeral states of being deems himself to be the best and thinks that he is not vile.

What is it but lack of consideration, when a man is proud, thinking ' It is I,' while his very form is inconstant and he is transitory and by nature subject to destruction ?

Passion *(kamaraga)* is the violent covert connate adversary, which strikes under the guise of friendship, like an evil-doing enemy.

The fire of passion and an ordinary fire are alike in their nature of burning, but when the fire of passion is blazing, the night will indeed be long.

But a fire is said not to have the same force as the fire of passion; for a fire is quenched by water, but the fire of passion not even by a whole lake.

When the forest has been burnt by fire, in time the forest trees will grow again, but when fools are burnt by the fire of passion, there is no birth to the Law.

By reason of passion man seeks pleasure and for the sake of pleasure does evil; through doing evil he falls into Hell. There is no enemy equal to passion.

From passion arises desire, and from desire attachment to the lusts. From the lusts man comes to suffering. There is no adversary equal to passion.

The fool takes no account of the great illness called passion, and...

Though a man may rid himself of passion by grasping its impermanence, its impurity, its nature as suffering and its absence of self, yet by reason of his perverted mind he becomes impassioned again.

Therefore he who can see a thing *(vastu)* as it really is *(yathabhutam)*, when attachment arises with regard to it, is said to be one who sees reality *(bhutadarsin)*.

Just as when one looks at the virtues (of an object), attachment arises, so, when one considers its demerits, anger is brought on.

Therefore he who wishes to suppress anger should not let himself be affected by aversion; for as smoke from fire, anger arises from aversion.

Anger is as old age to the beautiful, as darkness to those who have eyes, the frustration of Law, Wealth and Pleasure, and the enemy of learning.

Anger is the chief darkness of the mind, the chief enemy of friendship, the destroyer of respect, the causer of degradation *(abhibhava?).*

Accordingly do not give way to anger, or if you do so, give it up. You should not follow after anger any more than you would after a snake whose nature it is to bite.

I deem him to be the true charioteer who steadfastly keeps anger in check with reins as though it were a chariot that had left the road; the other kind merely holds the reins.

Whoever wishes to be angry and does not wish to suppress its birth, afterwards When his anger passes away, he is burnt as if by touching fire.

When man gives birth to anger, his own mind is burnt up first; afterwards, as the anger increases, others may be burnt by it or they may not.

What is the good of malevolence towards those of one's enemies who have bodies, seeing that the world (of embodied beings) is oppressed (already) by the calamities of disease, &c. ?

Therefore knowing the world to be subject to suffering, you should cultivate benevolence and compassion for all beings in order to restrain anger."

Thus the Buddha, seeing them at that time to be full of sin, had compassion on them and reproved them with His sermon.

Just as, when people are ill, the doctor prescribes medicine for them according to their constitutions, in order to cure the disease.

So the Sage, knowing the dispositions of beings who are afflicted by the diseases of passion, old age, &c., gave them the medicine of knowledge of the real truth.

The Licchavis were delighted with such a sermon from the Sage and did reverence to Him with their heads, so that their jewelled crests hung down.

Then joining the palms of their hands and slightly inclining their bodies, they requested the Buddha to visit them, just as the gods requested Brhaspati.

The Sage, informing them that Amrapali's turn came first, explained that those of low degree should not be deprived of their rights in favour of the nobles.

On learning that the woman had forestalled them, they did much reverence to the Tathagata and returned to their natural frame of mind (i.e. wrathfulness).

But on the Omniscient's teaching them, they gained calmness of mind, just as the poison of snakes abates with the well-spoken spells of sages.

When the night had passed, Amrapali entertained Him, and (He went on) to the village of Venumati (to pass the rainy season there).

After passing the rainy season there, the Great Sage returned to Vaisali and sat down on the bank of Markata's pool.

He sat down by the root of a tree, and, as He shone there, Mara appeared in the grove and, approaching Him, said:—

"Formerly, O Sage, on the bank of the Nairanjana when I said to You, 'You have fulfilled Your task, enter Nirvana,' You made reply there:—

'I shall not enter Nirvana till I have given security to the afflicted and caused them to abandon the sins.'

Now many have attained salvation, or similarly wish to do so or will do so. Therefore enter Nirvana."

Then on hearing these words, the Best of Arhats said to him, "In three months' time I shall enter Nirvana, be not then impatient."

Then knowing his desire to have been fulfilled by the promise, he disappeared from there, greatly exulting.

Then the Great Seer entered with such force of yoga into concentration of mind that He gave up the bodily life due to Him *(bhutapurva?)* and continued to live in an unprecedented way by the might of His spiritual power.

At the moment that He abandoned His bodily life, the earth staggered like a drunken woman, and great firebrands fell from the quarters, like a line of stones from Meru, when it is coloured with fire.

Similarly Indra's thunderbolts flashed unceasingly on all sides, full of fire *(agnigarbha)* and accompanied by lightning; and flames blazed everywhere, as if wishing to burn up the world at the end of the aeon.

The mountains lost their peaks and scattered abroad heaps of broken trees, while drums in the sky gave forth discordant *(visama)* sounds, like caverns filled with the wind.

Then at that moment of universal commotion in the world of men, in heaven and in the sky, the Great Sage emerged from His deep concentration and uttered these words:—

"My body with its age released is like a chariot whose axle has been broken, and I continue to carry it on by My own power. Together with My years I am released from the bond of existence, as a bird when hatching breaking the egg."

24

COMPASSION FOR THE LICCHAVIS

Thereon, when Ananda saw the earthquake, his hair stood on end; and in his perturbation *(agatavega)* at what it could be, he trembled and was distressed.

He asked the Omniscient, the Knower of causers, what was the cause of it. The Sage then said to him with the voice of a maddened bull:—

"The reason for this earthquake is that I have cut off My days on earth; My life is fixed *(adhistha)* at three months from now."

Ananda, hearing this, was deeply moved, and his tears flowed, as gum flows from a sandalwood-tree when a mighty elephant breaks it down.

He was grieved, because the Buddha was his kinsman and his Guru; and, mourning miserably, he lamented in his wretchedness:—

"On hearing my Master's decision, my body sinks as it were, I have lost my bearings, and the teaching of the Law that I have heard is confused.

Alas ! The Tathagata, praised of men *(narasamsa)*, is speedily going to Nirvana, like a fire quickly extinguished for men who are perished with cold and whose garments are worn out.

The guide points out the path to embodied beings lost in the great forest of the sins and disappears all at once.

Men travel on a far road, overcome with thirst, and then the pool of cool water on their way suddenly dries up.

The Eye of the world, which is limpid and has dark-blue eyelashes, which sees the past, the present and the future, and which is wide open with knowledge, is about to close.

Verily, when the crop springs up and is withering for want of water, a cloud gives a shower and at once passes away *(majj)*.

The lamp that shines on all sides for beings going astray on the road by reason of the darkness of ignorance, is very suddenly extinguished."

Then seeing Ananda to be thus troubled in mind with grief, the Chief of comforters, the Best of those who know the truth, explained the truth to him:—

"Recognise, Ananda, the real nature of the world and be not grieved. For this world is an aggregation, and therefore impermanent because its state is compound *(samskrta)*.

I have told you before that you should look on creatures who delight in the pairs *(dvandvarama)* with compassion entirely devoid of affection.

Whatever is born is compound and ephemeral; being dependent on a support, it has no self-dependence. It is impossible then for anyone to attain the state of permanence.

It beings on earth were permanent, the state of active being *(pravrtti)* would not be subject to change; and what need then of salvation ? For the end would be (the same as) the beginning.

Or again what is the desire you and other beings have for Me ? For you have done without Me that for which effort is made.

I have steadfastly explained the path to yon in its entirety; you, as disciples, should understand that the Buddhas withhold nothing.

Whether I remain or whether I pass to peace, there is only one thing, namely that the Tathagatas are the Body of the Law *(dharmakaya)*; of what use is this mortal body to you ?

Since at the time of My passing My lamp has been lit with full devotion (?) through perturbation of mind *(samvega)* and heedfulness *(apramada)*, therefore the light of the Law goes on for ever.

You should know it as your lamp, devoting steadfast

energy to it; and, freed from the pairs, recognise your goal *(svartka)* and let not your mind be a prey to other things.

You should know that the lamp of the Law is the lamp of mystic wisdom *(prajna)*, with which the skilful and learned man dispels ignorance, as a lamp the darkness.

For obtaining the highest good, there are four spheres of action *(gocara)*, to wit, the body, sensation, the mind and absence of self.

There is no attachment to the body, for him who sees the impurity in the body, enveloped as it is with bones, skin, blood, sinews, flesh, hair, &c.

The idea of pleasure is overcome by him who sees that the sensations are but suffering, each arising from their respective causes.

For him who sees with tranquil mind the birth, duration and decay of the (*mental*) elements *(dharma)*, the grasping of wrong views *(graha)* is for ever rejected.

For him who sees that the components *(skandha)* arise from causes, the thought of self which gives rise to the belief in an ego ceases to be active.

This is the only road to take to annihilate suffering; accordingly remain attentive on the Path with respect to these four.

Accordingly, when I pass to the Beyond, those who take their stand on this will obtain the excellent stage that does not pass away, the final beatitude."

Thus the Teacher preached to Ananda; and the Licchavis, hearing the news, came there hurriedly out of devotion to Him.

Their minds were carried away by bitterness (*samtapa*) by reason of their pity and of their devotion to the Seer, and at the news they speedily abandoned alike the affairs on which they were engaged (?) and their usual pomp *(rddhi)*.

Wishing to speak to the Master, they bowed and stood on one side, and the Master, the Sage, knowing their wish to speak, addressed them thus:—

"I know all that has come into your minds regarding Me; you, still the same, yet as if changed by grief, have now become self-confident (?).

Still abiding in the company *(varga?)* of sovereignty, you now have entirely present in you both outward brilliance *(dipti?)* and knowledge of the Law.

If indeed by hearing a little you have acquired knowledge from Me, calm yourselves and be not distressed at My passing.

Inasmuch as the states of being are impermanent and compounds, they are ephemeral, subject to change, without substance and not to be relied on; they do not remain stable in the least degree.

Vasistha, Atri and others, and whoever else was ascetic *(urdhvaretus)* came under the dominion of Time. Existence here is pernicious.

Mandhatr, the ruler of the earth, and Vasu, the peer of Vasava, and Nabhag'a, whose lot was noble *(mahabhaga)*, became one with the elements.

Yayati too, who walked in the path, Bhagiratha of the magnificent chariot, Kurus who achieved blame and ill fame, Rama, Girirajas (?), Aja.

These majestic *(mahatman)* royal seers and many others like Great Indra went to destruction; for there is no one who is not subject to destruction.

The sun falls from his station, the gods of wealth came to earth, hundreds of Indras have passed away; for no one exists for ever.

All the other Sambuddhas, after illuminating the world, entered Nirvana, like lamps whose oil is exhausted.

All the great-souled beings, who ,will become Tathagatas in the future, will also enter Nirvana like fires whose fuel has been consumed.

Therefore I too should go on, like an ascetic in the forest who seeks liberation; for there is no reason why I should drag out a useless corporeal existence *(namarupa)*.

Since it is My intention to depart from this pleasant *(ramaniya)* Vaisali, in which there are some to be converted, do ye never follow another faith *(anyamanas?)*.

Therefore know the world to be without refuge, helpless

and ephemeral; and walking in passionlessness obtain perturbation of mind *(samvega)*.

Thus to put it briefly, in due course when the Tathagata is no more seen, proceed in the direction of Kubera (i.e. the north), like the sun in the month of Jyestha."

Thereon the Licchavis followed Him with eyes full of tears; and, with stout arms laden with ornaments, they joined the palms of their hands and lamented:—

"Alas ! The Master's body, like refined gold and having the thirty-two marks, will break up. The Compassionate One is impermanent too.

The wretched, calves, who have not yet attained reason, are thirsty for lack of milk, and the milch-cow of knowledge, Alas ! too quickly deserts them.

The Sage is the sun whose light of knowledge has dispelled the darkness of delusion for men without a lamp, and suddenly this sun will set.

While the stream of ignorance flows hither and thither in the world, the far-reaching embankment of the Law is breached too soon.

The great compassionate Physician has the medicine of excellent knowledge, yet, abandoning the world which is sick with mental diseases, He will depart.

The flag of Indra, garnished with the diamonds of the mind and decorated with the ornaments of mystic wisdom, will fall, while people still thirst for it in the feast.

Seeing that for the world, whose lot is suffering and which is bound with the fetters of the cycle of existence, this is the door of release, Death will close it fast."

Thus the Licchavis lamented, their eyes turbid with tears; and when they followed after Him, the Sage turned them back again.

Then knowing the Sage's decision they became calm and in the deepest grief determined to return.

As, fair as the golden mountain, they did obeisance to the Sage's feet, they resembled *karnikara* trees, when their flowers are being shaken by the wind.

With hearts attached to Him, their feet too lagged, and

like waves moving against the stream, they turned back without moving onward.

Without joy in that for which they had had reverence, and without reverence for that in which they had rejoiced, their joy in, and reverence for, the Sage were immovable.

"Like mighty bulls, when the herd-bull has gone away from the forest, they kept on stopping and gazing repeatedly at the Holder of the Ten Forces.

Then with their minds dwelling on the Tathagata and with their bodies too bereft of brilliance, they went on foot in grief, as if proceeding to the final bath of a funeral ceremony *(apasnata)*.

The Licchavis returned to their palaces with their faces working with grief, though they had overcome their foes with bows whose arrows never missed the mark, though they were proud and strong and . . ., and though they sought sovereignty in the world and had great command over the means of pleasure.

25

TOWARDS NIRVANA

When the Sage departed for His Nirvana, Vaisali, like the sky overspread with darkness on the eclipse of the sun, no longer appeared brilliant.

Though beautiful and free from pride, though delightful *(ramaniya)* in all parts, it did not shine because of its burning sorrow *(samtapa),* like a woman whose husband has died.

Like beauty without learning, like knowledge without virtue, like intelligence without power of expression, like power of expression without education *(samskara),*

Like sovereignty (*sri*) without good conduct, like affection without faith, like good fortune *(laksmi?)* without energy, like action without religion *(dharma).*

At that time . . ., it was not brilliant because of its grief, like the earth with its dried up rice-crop, when the rain fails in the autumn.

There from grief no one cooked or ate his food; they all wept, as they recounted the fame of the famous Sage.

With others neither saying, nor doing, nor thinking anything at all, the city was given up to one single business, mourning and weeping.

Then the Senapati Simha, distressed with grief for all his firmness and thinking on the Chief . . ., uttered these laments:—

" He overcame the heretical systems and taught the good path, Himself proceeding on such a path. Now He has gone never to return.

The Lord *(natha)* is abandoning the world which is destroyed by afflictions and is without brilliance, and is turning the people into orphans; so He goes to obtain peace *(sama)*,

As the strength of the body *(ojas?)* with the lapse of time, so my steadfastness is destroyed, now that the excellent Guru, the Master of Yoga, is on His way to the final peace.

As king Nahusa lost his magic powers and fell from heaven, so the earth without Him is an object of pity, and I know not what is to be done.

To whom now shall people resort for the solution of their doubts, as one resorts to water when distressed by heat, or to a fire, if afflicted with cold ?

When the Sage, the spiritual Director of the world *(lakacarya)*, He Who is the Bellows of the final good, like bellows for blowing up a fire, is lost, the Law will be lost too.

Who is there like Him to break the mighty revolving wheel of suffering for beings, who are subject by nature to disease and death and are fettered by lack of discipline or wrong discipline?

Who else is able by his word to animate men in whom passion is born with mirth, like a cloud at the end of spring animating the dried up *sinduvara* plants ?

When the Omniscient Guru, solid as Meru, shall pass away, who in the world will have the wisdom that will make him an object of trust ?

The world of the living, being deluded, is born but to die, as the condemned criminal is made intoxicated and then led out to execution.

As a tree is cloven by a sharp saw, so this world is cloven by the saw of destruction.

Though the excellent spiritual Director of the world has the strength of knowledge and has entirely burnt up the sins, yet He is going to destruction.

He Who with the mighty boat of knowledge rescues men from the ocean of existence, whose billows are desires and whose water ignorance, and in which are the creatures of false views and the fish of passion *(rajas)*.

He Who cuts down with the great weapon of knowledge the tree of existence, whose boughs are old age and whose flowers disease, whose root is death and whose shoots rebirths *(bhava)*;

The cool water of Whose knowledge puts out the fire of the faults, which is produced from the rubbing-sticks of ignorance with the flames of passion and the fuel of the objects of sense;

He Who has taken the path of quietude, Who has abandoned the great darkness (of ignorance), Who, knowing the supreme knowledge of the final beatitude, has lovingly taught it;

The Omniscient, Who has gone too to the end of all the sins and looks benignly on all, Who works everyone benefit, He is going away to abandon everything.

If the Great Sage, Whose voice is soft and clear and Whose arms long, comes to an end, who will be able to avoid coming to an end ?

Therefore the wise man should quickly resort to the Law, as a caravan-merchant, who is lost in the wilderness, on seeing water, quickly resorts to it.

He who is not asleep to the Law, knowing impermanency to be an evil which makes no distinctions for the purpose of destruction, is not asleep, even though lying down."

Then Simha, the man-lion, the eater (?) of knowledge, denounced the evils of birth and praised the destruction of existence.

Desiring to give up the root of existence, to undertake good vows, and to control his restless mind, he desired to abide in the path of beatitude.

Desiring to walk in the path of quietude, to escape from the ocean of existence, and to be ever charitable, he desired to cut off rebirth.

At the time when the Sage wished to enter Nirvana, he gave in charity and abandoned pride, he meditated on the Law and reached quietude, and thus he treated the earth as an empty stage.

Then the Sage, turning round with His entire body like a king of elephants and looking at the city, uttered these words:—

"O Vaisali, I shall not see you again in the period of life that still remains to Me; for I am going to Nirvana."

Then seeing that they were following Him full of faith and desiring the Law, the Sage dismissed them, whose minds still tended to the continuance of activity.

Then in due course the Teacher proceeded to Bhoganagara, and, staying there, the Omniscient said to His followers:—

"After I have passed away to-day, you must fix your best attention on the Law. It is your highest goal; anything else is but toil.

Whatever is not entered in the Sutras or does not appear in the Vinaya is contrary to My principles *(nyaya?)* and should not be accepted by any means.

For that is not the Law nor the Vinaya nor My words; though many people say it, it is to be rejected as the saying of darkness.

The preaching of the pure is to be accepted, for that is the Law, the Vinaya, My words; and not to abide in it is backsliding.

Therefore what is to be believed is stated succinctly in My Sutras. Who does (i.e. follows?) them is to be trusted, and apart from this there is no authority.

Out of delusion there will arise doctrines of the Law, laying down what is not the Law, through uncertainty and ignorance about these subtle views of Mine.

Either by views associated with darkness, or from ignorance of the distinctions, just as men are cheated by brass which looks like gold.

Accordingly that which is not the Law, but merely a counterfeit of the Law, is a deception, arising from lack of mystic wisdom or from failure to grasp the real truth.

Therefore you should test it in the proper form *(nyayatah)* by means of the Vinaya and Sutras, just as a goldsmith tests gold by filing, cutting and heating it.

Those are not wise men who do not know the doctrines *(sastra);* they determine that as the course to be followed *(nyaya)* which is not the right course and see in the right course the wrong one.

Therefore it is to be accepted with the right hearing according to the meaning and the word; for he who grasps the doctrine wrongly hurts himself, as one who grasps a sword wrongly (by the blade) cuts himself.

He who construes the -words wrongly finds the meaning with difficulty, as a man at night finds a house with difficulty, if he has not been there before and the way is winding.

When the meaning is lost, the Law is lost, and when the Law is lost, capacity is lost; therefore he is intelligent whose mind abides unperverted in the meaning."

After the Gracious One had uttered these words, He went on in due time to the town of Papa, where the Mallas did him all honour.

Then the Holy One took His last meal in the house of the excellent Cunda, who was devoted to Him, doing so for his (Cunda's) sake, not for His own support.

Then, after the Tathagata with His company of disciples had eaten, He preached the Law to Cunda and went to Kusinagara.

Thus accompanied by Cunda He crossed the river Iravati(?) and betook Himself to a grove of that city, which had a peaceful lotus-pool.

He Who shone like gold bathed in the Hiranyavati, and then He thus ordered the mourning Ananda, the joy of the world *(lokanandana*?):—

"Ananda, prepare a place for Me to lie on between the twin *sala* trees; this day in the latter part of the night the Tathagata will enter Nirvana."

When Ananda heard these words, a film of tears spread over his eyes; he prepared a place for the Buddha to lie on, and having done so, informed Him of it, lamenting.

Then the Best of the two-footed approached His final couch, in order never to wake again and to put an end to all suffering.

In the presence of His disciples He lay down on His right side, pillowing His head on His hand and crossing His legs.

Then at that moment there the birds uttered no cries and sat with bodies all relaxed, as if fixed in trance.

Then the trees, with their restless leaves unstirred by breezes, shed discoloured flowers, as if weeping.

Like travellers coming in sight of their resting-place, when the maker of day stands on the Sunset mountain, so, gazing at the Sage on His couch, they quickly came in sight of the good goal.

Then the Omniscient, lying on His last resting-place, said in His compassion to the tear-stained Ananda:—

"Tell the Mallas, Ananda, of the time of My entering Nirvana; for if they do not witness the Nirvana, afterwards they will deeply regret it."

Then Ananda, swooning with tears, obeyed the order, and told the Mallas that the Sage was lying on His final bed.

Then at that time on hearing Ananda's words, overcome by distress, they issued forth from the town, like bulls from a mountain in fear of a lion, mourning and raining down tears from their eyes.

In their lack of joy their clothes were disordered and tumbled, and their headdresses shook with the agitation of their steps. Then they came to that grove, a prey to affliction like the dwellers in heaven when their merit is exhausted.

Coming there thus they saw the Sage, and on seeing Him, their faces were covered with tears, as they did obeisance; having paid their reverence, they stood there, their hearts burning within them. As they stood there, the Sage spoke to them:—

"It is not proper to grieve in the hour of joy. Despair is out of place, resume your composure. That remote *(atidurlabha)* goal, for which I have longed for many aeons, is now come near to Me.

That goal is most excellent, without the elements of earth, water, fire, wind and space, blissful and immutable, beyond the objects of sense, peaceful, inviolable *(aharya)*, and in which there is neither birth nor passing away. On hearing of it, there is no room for grief.

Formerly at the time of Illumination in Gaya I put away from Me the causes of evil existence as if they were snakes; but this body, this dwelling house of the acts accumulated in the past, has survived till to-day.

Is it proper to sorrow for Me that you weep, when this aggregate, the great storehouse of suffering, is passing away, when the great danger of existence is being extirpated and I am departing from the great suffering?"

When they heard the Sage of the Sakyas announce with a voice like a cloud that the time had come for Him to enter on peace, their mouths opened with the desire to speak, and the oldest of them uttered these words:—

"Is sorrow fitting that you all weep? The Sage is like a man who has escaped from a house blazing with fire, and when even the chief of the gods should so look on it, how much more should men do so ?

But this causes us grief that the Lord, the Tathagata, on entering Nirvana, will be no more seen; when in the desert the good guide dies, who will not be sorely afflicted ?

Surely men become objects of derision, like those who come away poor from a goldmine, if, having seen the Guru, the Omniscient Great Seer, in person, they do not win to the higher path *(visesa).*"

Thus the Mallas spoke much that was to the point, folding their hands in devotion like sons, and the Best of the high-souled replied to them with words of excellent meaning directed to the highest good and to tranquillity:—

"So indeed is it the case that salvation does not come from the mere sight of Me without strenuous practice in the methods of yoga; he who thoroughly considers this My Law is released from the net of suffering, even without the sight of Me.

Just as a man does not overcome disease by the mere sight of the physician without resort to medicine, so he who does not study *(bhavaya)* this My knowledge does not overcome suffering by the mere sight of Me.

In this world the self-contrftlled man who sees my Law may live far away in point of space, yet he sees Me; while he who is not active in concentration *(parayana)* on the highest good may dwell at My side and yet be far distant.

Therefore be ever energetic and control your minds; with diligence practise the deeds that lead to good. For life is like the flame of a lamp in the wind, flickering and subject to much suffering."

Thus they were instructed by the Seer, the Best of beings, and with harassed minds and tears pouring down from their eyes, they returned to Kusinagara reluctantly and helplessly, as if crossing the middle of a river against the stream.

26

THE MAHAPARINIRVANA

Then Subhadra, a holder of the triple staff, who was properly endowed, with good virtue and did no hurt to any being, desired to see the Blessed One in order to obtain salvation as a mendicant. So he said to Ananda, the causer of universal delight:—

"I have heard that the Sage's hour for entering Nirvana has come, and therefore I desire to see Him; for it is as hard in this world to see One Who has penetrated to the highest Law as it is to see the moon on the day it is new.

I desire to see your Teacher, Who is about to proceed to the end of all suffering; let Him not pass away without my seeing Him, like the sun setting in a sky veiled by clouds."

Then Ananda's mind was filled with emotion, for he thought the wandering ascetic *(parivrajaka)* had come in order to dispute under the pretext of a desire for the Law; and with face covered with tears, be said, "It is not the time."

Then He, Who shone like the moon, knowing the dispositions of men, recognized that the ascetic's eye was opening like a petal, and He said, "Do not hinder the twice-born, Ananda, since I was born for the good of the world."

There at Subhadra, comforted and highly delighted, approached the Srighana, the Doer of the highest good; then as befitted the occasion, in a quiet way he greeted Him and spoke these words:–

"It is said that You have gained a path of Salvation other than that of philosophers (*pariksaka*) like myself; therefore explain it to me, for I wish to accept it. My desire to see You arises from affection, not from desire for disputation."

Then the Buddha explained the Eightfold Path to the twice-born, who had come to Him; and he listened to it, like a man who has lost his way listens to the correct directions, and he... fully considered it.

Then he per-ceived that the final good was not obtained on the other paths he had previously followed, and winning to a path he had not seen before, he put away those other paths which are accompanied by darkness in the heart.

For in those paths, it is said, by obtaining darkness (*tamas*) accompanied by passion (*rajas*) evil (*akusala*) deeds are heaped up, while by passion associated with goodness (*sattva*) good (*kusala*) deeds are extended.

With goodness increasing through learning, intelligence and effort, and by reason of the effect of the act being destroyed through the disappearance of darkness and passion, the effect of the act becomes exhausted; and that power of the act they postulate is said to be the product of nature.

For in the world they attribute darkness and passion, which delude the mind, to Nature. Since Nature is acknowledged to be permanent, those two equally do not cease to exist, being necessarily also permanent.

Even if by uniting oneself with goodness those two cease to exist, they will come into being again under the compulsion of time, just as water, which gradually becomes ice at night, returns to its natural state in the course of time.

Since goodness is permanent by nature, therefore learning, wisdom and effort have no power to increase it; and since it does not increase, the other two are not destroyed, and since they are not destroyed, there is no final peace.

Previously he had held birth to be by Nature, now he saw that there was no salvation in that doctrine; for since one exists by Nature, how can there be final release any more than a blazing fire can he stopped from giving out light?

Seeing the Buddha's path to be the real truth, he held the world to depend on desire; if that is destroyed, there is religious peace *(sama)*, for with the destruction of the cause the result also is destroyed.

Previously he had held with respect to that which is manifested *(vyakta)* that the "self " is other than the body and is not subject to change; now that he had listened to the Sage's words he knew the world to be without "self " and not to be the effect of " self."

Realising that birth depends on the interrelation of many elements *(dharma)* and that nothing is self-dependent, he saw that the continuance of active being *(pravrtti)* is suffering and that the cessation thereof *(nivrtti)* is freedom from suffering.

Since he considered that the world is a product, he gave up the doctrine of annihilation, and since he knew that the world passes away, he speedily gave up without shrinking *(dhira)* the view of its permanence.

Hearing and accepting the Great Seer's teaching, he thus gave up on the spot his former views; for he had formerly prepared himself *(yarikarma kr)*, so that he quickly adhered to the good Law.

His mind was filled with faith and, obtaining the best, he reached the peaceful immutable stage; and therefore, as he gazed gratefully on the Sage lying there, he formed this resolution.

"It is not proper for me to stay and see the venerable excellent Lord enter Nirvana; I shall myself go straight to the final end, before the compassionate Master passes to Nirvana."

Then he did obeisance to the Sage, and assuming a moveless posture snakewise, he passed in a moment into the peace of Nirvana, like a cloud dissipated by the wind.

Thereon the Sage, the Knower of rites, gave orders for the rite of his cremation, saying, "He has gone to the end, the last disciple of the Great Seer Who has noble disciples."

Then when the first part of the night had passed away, and the moon had eclipsed the light of the stars, and the groves were without a sound as if asleep, He Whose compassion was great instructed His disciples:—

"When I have gone to the Beyond, you should treat the Pratimoksa as your spiritual director *(acarya)*, as your lamp, as your treasure. That is your teacher, under whose dominion you should be, and you should repeat it just as you did in My lifetime.

In order to purify your bodily and vocal actions give up all worldly concerns *(vyavahara)*, and, as from grasping a fire, refrain from accepting lands, living beings, grain, treasure and the rest.

The proper means of livelihood is to abstain from the cutting and felling of what grows on the earth, from digging and ploughing the surface of the ground, and from medicine and astrology.

There is neither moderation nor contentment nor life in resorting to the knowledge of go-betweens, in the practice of charms and philtres, in not being open and candid, or in the attainments not forbidden by the Law.

In this way the Pratimoksa is the summary of the discipline (sila) the root of liberation; from it arise the concentrated meditations, all forms of knowledge and the final goals.

For this reason he has the Law, in whom is found pure inviolable discipline, neither rent nor destroyed; and without it all these (advantages) are absent, for discipline is the support of good qualities.

When discipline abides undestroyed and purified, there is no activity in the spheres of the senses; for, just as cattle are kept from the crops by a stick, so the six senses should be guarded *(samvrta)* with firmness.

But the other man who lets the horses of his senses loose among the objects of sense is carried away and obtains no satisfaction from them. Like one carried out of the road *(kumarga)* by runaway horses, he incurs disaster for their sake.

Some men in this world suffer bitterly by falling into the hands of great enemies, but those, who from delusion fall into the power of the objects of sense, become subject to suffering, whether they will or no *(avasa)*, in their futare lives as well as in this.

Therefore recourse should no more he had to the senses than to evil *(visama)* enemy kings; for after taking one's pleasure of the senses in this world, one sees in the world the executioner of the senses.

One should not tear tigers or snakes or blazing fires or enemies in the world so much as one's own restless mind, which sees the honey hut overlooks the danger *(sanka)*.

The mind wanders in all directions as it wills, like a mad elephant unrestrained by the iron ankus or like a monkey *(sakhamrga)* gambolling in the trees; no occasion should he given to it far restlessness.

When the mind is a law unto itself, there is no quietude, but when it comes to a stand, the task is done. Therefore strive with all your might that these minds of yours may desist from restlessness.

Observe exact measure in eating, as you would for doses of physic, and do not feel repulsion or desire towards it, only taking so much as is necessary for satisfying hunger and for maintaining the body.

As in the garden the bees do not destroy the flowers in sipping their juice, so you should practise alms-begging at the proper time without ruining other believers.

The rule that a load must always be put on correctly applies equally to an ox and to an alms-giver. The load falls off from being wrongly attached in this world, and the giver is in the same case as the ox.

Pass the entire day and also the first and last watches of the night in the practice of yoga, and lie down in the middle watch, full of awareness so that the time of sleep does not bring on calamity.

For when the world here is being burnt up by the fire of Time, is it proper to sleep for the whole night ? When the sins, which strike down like enemies, abide in the heart, who would go to sleep?

Therefore you should sleep, after exorcizing with knowledge and the repetition of sacred texts the snakes of the sins which reside in the heart, as one does black snakes in a house by magic and charms; besides it is a question of self-respect (*hri*).

Self-respect is an ornament and the best elothing, the ankus for those who have strayed from the path. Such being the case, you should act with self-respect; for to be devoid of self-respect is to be devoid of the virtues.

A man is (honoured) to the extent to which he has self-respect, and he, who is lacking in self-respect and who is devoid of discrimination between what is what is not his real good, is on a level with the brute beasts.

Even should anyone cut off your arms and limbs with a sword, you should not cherish sinful thoughts about him or speak unforgiving (*asanta?*) words; for such action is an obstruction to you alone.

There are no austerities equal to forbearance, and he who has forbearance has strength and fortitude, whereas those who cannot tolerate harsh treatment from others do not follow the way of those who lay down the Law, nor are they saved.

Do not allow the slightest opening to anger, which ruins the Law and destroys fame, and which is the enemy of beauty and a fire to the heart; there is no enemy to the virtues like unto it.

While anger is contrary to the profession of religion (*pravrajya*) like the fire of lightning to cold water, it is not contrary to the life of the householder; for the latter are full of passion and have taken no vows about it.

If pride arises in your heart, it must be controverted by touching your head shorn of its beautiful locks, by looking on your dyed clothes and your begging bowl, and by reflecting on the conduct and occupations (*karmanta*) of others.

If worldly men who are proud (strive) to overcome pride, how much more should those do so, whose heads are shaven, who have directed themselves to salvation, and who eat the bread of mendicancy and have proved themselves.

Since deceitfulness and the practice of the Law are incompatible, do not resort to crooked ways. Deceitfulness and false pretences *(maya)* are for the sake of cheating, but for those who are given to the Law there is no such thing as cheating.

The suffering which comes to him whose desires are great does not come to him whose desires are small. Therefore smallness of desire *(alpecchata)* should be practised, and especially so by those who seek for the perfection of the virtues.

He who does not fear the rich at all is not afraid of the sight of stingy people; for he obtains salvation, whose desires are small and who is not cast down on hearing that there is nothing for him.

If you desire salvation, practise contentment; with contentment there is bliss here and it is the Law. The contented sleep peacefully even on the ground, the discontented are burnt up even in Paradise.

The discontented man, however rich, is always poor, and the contented man, however poor, is always rich. The discontented man, seeking the beloved objects of sense, creates suffering for himself by toiling to obtain satiety.

Those who desire to obtain the highest bliss of peace should not give themselves up to the pleasures in such degree. For even Indra and the other gods envy the man in the world who is solely devoted to tranquillity.

Attachment is the roosting-tree *(vasavrksa)* of suffering; therefore give up attachment, whether to relations or to strangers. He who has many attachments in the world is stuck fast in suffering, like a decrepit elephant in the mud.

A stream, whose waters ever flow, however softly, in time wears away the surface of the rock. Energy finds nothing impossible of attainment. Therefore be strenuous and do not put down your loads.

The man who stops repeatedly in drilling with fir-sticks finds it hard to get fire from wood, but by the application of energy is it comes easily. Therefore where there is diligence, the task is in accomplished.

When awareness *(smrti)* is present, the faults do not enter into activity; there is no friend or protector equal to awareness, and if awareness is lost, all certainly is lost. Therefore do not lose hold of awareness directed towards the body.

The firm in mind, putting on the armour of awareness towards the body, conduct themselves in the battlefield of the objects of sense like heroes, who gird on their armour and plunge fearlessly into the ranks of their foes.

Therefore, keeping your feelings level and restraining your minds, know the origin and passing away of the world and practise concentration. For no mental ills touch him who has obtained concentration of mind.

Just as men diligently make embankments for holding up water that is overflowing, so concentration is declared to be like the embankment for bringing the water of knowledge to stand.

The wise man *(prajna)*, who abides giving away his possessions and entirely devoted to this Law in his heart, is saved; how much more then should the mendicant, who has no home, be saved ?

Mystic wisdom is the boat on the great ocean of old age and death, a lamp, as it were, in the darkness of delusion, the medicine that smites all illnesses, the sharp axe that cuts down the trees of the sins.

Therefore practise learning, knowledge and meditation *(bhavana)* for the increase of mystic wisdom; for he who has the eye that is of the nature of mystic wisdom, though without ocular vision, has indeed sight.

Although a man has left his home, yet, if he is engaged in the varied activities of the mind, he is not saved; those who desire to obtain the supreme tranquillity should know this and become free from all activities.

Therefore adhere to heedfulness *(apramada)* as to a guru, and avoid heedlessness as an enemy. By heedfulness Indra obtained sovereignty, by heedlessness the arrogant Asuras came to destruction.

I have done all that should be done by a compassionate sympathetic Master, Who aims at others' good; do you apply yourselves *(pranidha?)* and bring your minds to tranquillity.

Then, wherever you may, on the mountains or in empty dwellings or in the forest, ever be strenuous in religious practice *(prayoga)* and do not give way to remorse *(pasacatparitapa).*

It is for the physician, after full consideration of their constitutions, to explain the proper medicines to his patients, but it is the sick man, not the physician, who is responsible for attending to their administration at the proper time.

When the guide has pointed out the magnificent straight level road which is free from danger, and those who hear him do not proceed along it but go to destruction, there is no debt in the way of instruction still due from the guide.

Whoever of you has any desire about My teaching of the Four Truths, suffering and the rest, let him confidently speak out to Me at once and cut off doubt *(ativimarsa?)."*

When the Great Seer thus spoke aloud, they were free from doubt and said nothing. The saintly *(krtin)* Aniruddha, penetrating their minds with his mind, then uttered these words:—

"Though the wind cease from movement, the sun become -cold and the moon hot, yet it is not possible to prove the four steps (of the Truths) to be false in the world.

What is declared to be suffering is not pleasure; there is no other producer of suffering than that which is its cause; liberation inevitably comes from suppression of the cause, and the path thereto is certainly the means.

Therefore, O Great-souled One, the disciples have no doubt about the Four Truths; but those who have not accomplished their object suffer, thinking that the Teacher is about to pass away.

Even he in this assembly, who from the newness of his vows had not yet seen the goal, sees it to-day in its entirety, as by a flash of lightning, through this Your sermon.

But even those, for whom there is nothing remaining to be done and who have crossed to the further shore of the ocean of existence, are anxious in heart on hearing that the perfect *(svalamkrta?)* Lord is about to pass away."

At these words of the noble *(arya)* Aniruddha, the Buddha, though He knew the matter, again took cognizance of it and addressed them affectionately, in order to strengthen the minds of the faithful:—

" Since a being may last for an aeon and yet must come to destruction, there is certainly no such thing as mutual union. Having completed the task both for Myself and for others, there is no gain in My further existence.

All those in the heavens and on earth, who were to be converted by Me, have been saved and set in the stream. Hereafter this My Law shall abide among men through the successive generations of mendicants.

Therefore recognize the true being of the world and be not anxious; for separation must be. Knowing the world to be of this nature, so strive that it may be thus no more.

When the darkness has been illuminated with the lamp of knowledge and the spheres of existence have been seen to be without substance, contentment ensues at the suppression of the life-force *(ayuh),* as at the cure of an illness.

Who is not pleased at the cessation of life, as at the destruction of calamity-causing enemies, when the stream of the ocean of existence called the body, which is to be abandoned with the opposites *(dvandva),* is cut off ?

Everything, whether moving or stationary, passes away; therefore take ye good heed. The time for My entering Nirvana has arrived. Do not lament; these are My last words."

Then the Best of those who know the trances entered the first trance at that moment, and emerging therefrom went on to the second, and so in due order He entered all of them without omitting any *(avikala?).*

Thereon having passed through all the trances, the group of nine attainments *(samapatti),* in the upward order, the Great Seer following the reverse order returned to the first trance again.

Emerging therefrom also, He rose in due order again to the fourth trance, and emerging from the practice of the fourth trance, He passed to realization of the eternal peace.

Thereon, as the Sage entered Nirvana, the earth quivered like a ship struck by a squall, and firebrands also fell from the sky, as if cast (?) by the elephants of the quarters.

A fire, without fuel or smoke and unfanned by the wind, arose burning the quarters, like a forest fire arising in the sky to burn the heavenly garden of Citraratha.

Fearsome thunderbolts fell, vomitting fire with hundreds of sparks, as if Indra was hurling them in his wrath, in order to overcome the Asuras in battle.

The winds blew violently, splintering the creepers and laden with dust, as if the peaks of the earth-bearing mountains had fallen when struck by raging tempests.

The moon's light waned, and it shone with feeble colourless beams, like a royal goose, when it is covered with muddy water and its body is surrounded by young reeds.

Though the sky was cloudless and the moon was up, unholy darkness spread over the quarters, and at that moment the rivers ran with boiling water as if overcome by grief.

Then the *sala* trees that grew near by bent down and showered beautiful flowers, growing out of due season, on to the Buddha's body to rest on the golden column (?) of His form.

In the sky the five-headed Nagas stood motionless, gazing on the Sage with devotion, their eyes reddened with grief, their hoods closed and their bodies kept in restraint.

In the affliction of their minds they gave vent to hot sighs, but, reflecting that the world is impermanent by nature, they refrained from grief and despised it.

In the divine abode the virtuous assembly of king Vaisravana, which was engaged in the practice of the Law of final beatitude, did not grieve or shed tears by reason of their attachment to the Law.

The holy (*krtin*) Suddhadhivasa deities, though they held the Great Seer in the utmost reverence, were composed and felt no agitation of mind; for they despised the nature of the world.

The gods, who rejoice in the good Law, the Gandharva

kings, the Naga kings and the Yaksas, stood in the sky, mourning and absorbed in uttermost grief as if confounded *(mahakula)*.

But the hosts of Mara, who had obtained his heart's desire, uttered loud laughs in their exultation, and showed their joy by gambols, hissing like snakes, dancing and the beating of tattoos on great drums, *mrdangas* and *patahas*.

Then on the Bull of seers passing to the Beyond, the world became like a mountain whose peak has been shattered by a thunderbolt, or a despondent elephant when his must has ceased, or a bull whose form is deprived of its hump.

From the loss of Him Who destroyed existence, the world became like the sky without the moon, or a pond whose lotuses have been withered by frost, or learning rendered futile by the absence of wealth.

27

EULOGY

Then a certain mighty inhabitant of heaven, bowing his head a little from out of the palace *(vimana)* of the . . . god, looked on the Omniscient for a moment and spoke:—

"Alas ! Since all states of being are impermanent and subject to the law of birth and the law of decay, suffering is the peculiar lot of those who are born. Thus peace comes only from the peace that leaves naught behind.

As water puts out fire, so the water of Time had to put out the Tathagata's fire, whose flames are knowledge, whose smoke renown, and which has burnt up without residue the fuel of existence."

Then another seer, resembling the best of seers, and who, though abiding in Paradise, was not drawn to its enjoyments, gazed on the Seer, the Arhat Who had obtained tranquillity; and steadfast as the lord of mountains, he uttered these words:—

"There is nothing in the world that does not go to destruction, nothing, too that has not gone, nothing that will not go, seeing that the incomparable Master, Who had reached the highest knowledge and knew the supreme goal, has gone to tranquillity.

The world of the living, whose eyes are inevitably blinded by delusion, is deprivted of this Leader, Whose mystic wisdom was purified and Who possessed the supreme sight; and losing its senses, it abides in the evil path."

Then on the Sage's passing to peace Aniruddha, who was not obstructed *(viruddha)* by the world, in whom attachment *(anurodha)* was destroyed, and who had annihilated *(niruddha)* birth, saw the world to be deprived of its light, and spoke thus with calmness of mind:—

"The wise man, who is exposed to the action of the factors *(samskara)*, should have no confidence at this time, when the great mountain of the Sage is struck by the fall of the thunderbolt of impermanence.

Alas ! The world, which is without substance or self and which is subject to the law of destruction, is called the world of the living, the world in which even the unassailable Lion, the Great Sage, after destroying the elephants of the sins, Himself goes to destruction.

The world is ever active and involved in passion; whose hand then now will give the great security, seeing that sharing the general lot (*sadharanatah?*) even the Tathagata has fallen(?) like a golden column ?

The elephant, the Sage, pulled up this tree of the sins, which has six seeds, one sprout, one offering (*bali*), six roots, five fruits, two boughs, three stems (?, *rasi)* and one trunk; yet here He lies.

The Sage has gone to peace, after conquering all His foes like a world-monarch, without attachment like a peacock in the dry season, having completed His journey like a steed, freed from birth like fire (without fuel).

The Guru sent forth His teachings, like the satisfying streams which the lord of heaven, the wielder of the thunderbolt, sends forth, when his eye waxes, and wandering over the earth like an ox affticted by the glare, He pervaded the quarters with His renown; yet here He lies.

The Sun fo men went out on His road, attended by the host of Vaisravana, the lord of wealth, and full of fame and brilliancy. He streamed forth gold like a great river (*sindhu*); yet He has set.

To-day when the Sage has entered into peace, the world shines no more, like the quarters invested with banks (*hara*) of fog, like the sun with its beams intercepted by masses of cloud, or like a fire without ghee, when the oblations are completed.

Being without crookedness (*granthi*), He took the (straight) road of truth; and being without ties (*granthi*), He obtained the Law of tranquillity. Now He has abandoned that aboded of suffering known as the body, though able by His spiritual power (*rddhi*) to maintain its existence.

After overcoming ignorance as the sun dispels the darkness, after allaying passion as a shower lays the dust, the Sage has gone as... went, never again to return to the revolving wheel of suffering.

He was born to destory the suffering of birth, to Him the world resorted for the sake of tranquillity, He shone with glorious brillianey, and He illuminated with acute (*visista*) intelligence.

He sent the people towards the final good, He overspread the earth with His noble virtues, His dear shining fame waxed, and even when dwelling in the palace, He waxed in renown.

In the extent of His learning He was not downcast at blame, He spoke with pity to men who were in distress, He rejected wrong food and did not consume it, and on meeting with good food He felt no enjoyment.

Keeping the restless senses in palace, He rightly did not abide in the objects to sense by reason of the strength of His faculties, and obtaining the good path unobtained by others, He tasted renunciation (*naiskramya?*), He Who knew the tastes.

He gave what had never been given before (by man), and His gifts were never prompted by desire for reward; He abandoned sovereignty with mind unmoved (?) and attracted the minds of the good with His virtues.

He guarded His restless eye with firmness and was accustomed to guard His mind with firm conduct. He guarded and increased the final good, and He felt no desire for any phenomenon (*dharma*) that arose.

He firmly abandoned evil deeds as being evil (*asubhatah?*) and rid Himself of the enemies, the faults, by the highest good. He entirely extirpated the vices by His intelligence, yet He has succumbed to ignoble impermanence.

He rightly followed the Law and joyfully grasped the best resolutions; yet He, the Lord Who had the treasures of knowledge, is dead (*gatasu*), like a fire the treasure of whose fuel (*sara*) is consumed.

The Guru is lying here, He Who excellently subdued the group of five with regard to the eight, Who saw the three, Who brought the triple conduct to an end, Who had the triple sight, Who guarded the one, Who obtained the one, Who perpended the one, Who abandoned the seven weighty ones *(guruni?)*.

He illumined the road for the sake of quietude and graciously caused good men to believe, He cut down the... trees of the sins and delivered the faithful from the spheres of existence.

With the nectar of His words He fully satisfied the world, and subdued anger by His forbearance. He made the assembly of His disciples to delight in the highest good, and introduced those who sought the highest good to subtle investigations.

He engendered the seed of the Law in those who were good, and brought them to the Noble Path, whose essence is the cause; though He did not teach outsiders *(anarya)* by the supermundane *(lokottara)* way, He did not set them in any path other than that of the good Law.

In Kasi He turned the Wheel of the Law and by His wisdom brought content to the world; He caused those who were to be converted to practise the way of the Law, and brought bliss to us for our good.

Others He caused to see the real truth that they had not yet seen, and He united the followers of the Law with the virtues. By refuting *(nigrah?)* the other systems and by argument He caused men to understand the meaning which is hard to grasp.

By teaching everything to be impermanent and without self and by denying the presence of the slightest happiness in the spheres of existence, He raised aloft the banner of His fame and overturned the lofty pillars of pride.

Censure never disturbed His mind, and in all matters He had no desire for worldly activities...

Himself crossing over, He caused the drowning to cross over too; Himself tranquillized, He brought tranquillity to those who were agitated; Himself liberated, He liberated those who were bound; Himself enlightened, He enlightened the delusion of others.

The Sage of sages, Who knew the right course *(nyaya)* and the wrong one, after favouring creation with right instruction, has passed away, as the Law passes away in that age of fear, when beings follow the wrong course and delight in so doing.

Overcoming the views of the world, yet attracting the gaze of the world, He fared in His gait like a cloud full of rain, like the forest of the earth-bearing mountain, like an old man in his glory, like a young man in his brilliancy.

...He followed the path of supreme quietude, and the world, which, full of faith, saw Him obtain quietude, is to-day like a loving man without his relative (or, father).

Even Mara, accompanied by his hosts and raging mightily to destroy Him, was no match for the Sage; yet to-day Mara, raging mightily to destroy Him, has been able by alliance with Death *(mara)* to lay Him low.

All beings, for whom the dangers of the cycle of existence are still unexhausted, are assembled together with the gods and are overwhelmed with suffering; for thus they have not obtained the excellent passage beyond grief.

Illuminating all beings He saw the world as though reflected in a mirror, and His divine hearing perceived all sounds, far and near, even up to the heavens.

He mounted to the starry mansions in the sky, He penetrated the earth too without obstruction, He walked on the water also without sinking and produced many transformations with His body.

He remembered too His many births, like a traveller the various stopping-places on the road, and with his mind He understood the various mental movements of others, which are beyond the sphere of sensory perception.

He behaved alike to everyone and was omniscient, He cut off all the infections and completed all the task, through knowledge He abandoned all the sins and obtained the perfect knowledge *(jnanatattva),* yet here He lies.

He converted those men whose minds were active *(patu),* and gradually stimulated torpid minds to activity. He made them abandon vice by understanding *(vidya)* of the Law. Who will now teach the Law for deathlessness?

Who will give the offering *(bali)* of the Law for the sake of tranquillity to the world, which is harassed and without hope ? Who, after completing his own task, will be so compassionate as to cut through the net of sin for others ?

Who will declare the good knowledge for the tranquillity of the world, which is absorbed *(parayana?)* in the ocean of the cycle of existence ? Who will declare the good knowledge for the happiness of the world, which is absorbed in ignorance *(ajnana)?*

The world without Him Who knew the world is like the day-maker without his light, or a great river deprived of its current, or a king who has lost his sovereignty.

The world, deprived of the Best of men, exists and yet is not, like learning *(vidya)* without intelligence, like investigation without discrimination, like a king without majesty, like the Law without forbearance.

The world, on losing the Blessed One, is like a chariot abandoned by the charioteer, or a boat by the steersman, or an army by the general, or a caravan by the leader, or a sick man by the physician.

To-day the affliction of those who desire salvation is like a cloudless sky in autumn without the moon, like the air when there is no breeze, like the suffering of those who would live (but are dying)."

Thus though he was an Arhat who had completed the good task, he spoke much about the evils of existence and the virtues of the Master; for he acted out of gratitude to the Guru.

Then those who had not put away passion shed tears,

and the company of mendicants, losing their steadfastness of mind, gave way to grief; but those wlio had completed the cycle reflected that it is the nature of the world to pass away and did not depart from self-control.

Then in due course the Mallas, hearing the news, came streaming forth quickly under the stress of calamity, and, like cranes overwhelmed by the might of a hawk, cried in their affliction, "Alas ! The Saviour !"

Because of the great darkness of their minds, when they saw the Sage lying there like the sun without its light, they wept and uttered loud lamentations in their devotion, like cattle when a lion has struck down the herd-ball.

Among those whose eyes were overcome by tears and who were mourning according to their faith and disposition, when the Guru of the Law passed to peace, there was a certain excellent majestic man, who delighted the Law; he then spoke these words:—

"He, Who woke up the world of the living when it was asleep, now lies on His last bed. This Banner, incarnating the Law, has fallen, like Indra's banner when the feast is over.

The Sun of the Tathagata, with the brilliancy of Enlightenment, the heat of energy, and the thousand rays of knowledge, dispelled the darkness of ignorance; now at Its setting It has again brought darkness over the world.

Inexorably now the Eye of the world is closed, Which saw the past, the present and the future; inexorably the Embankment has been breached, Which saved us from the rolling billows of the great ocean of suffering."

Thus some wailed piteously there, others brooded, bowed down like chariot-horses; some uttered cries, others flung themselves on the ground. Each man behaved in accordance with his nature *(sattvd).*

Then in due course the weeping Mallas, with arms like the trunks of mighty elephants, placed the Seer on an unused priceless bier of ivory inlaid with gold.

Then with ceremonial that befitted the occasion they did Him reverence with entrancing garlands of many kinds and with the most excellent perfumes, and then with affection and devotion they all took hold of the bier.

Then tender-bodied maidens, with tinkling anklets and copper-stained hands, held over it a priceless canopy, like a cloud white with flashes of lightning.

Similarly some of the men held up umbrellas with white garlands, while others waved white yaks' tails set in gold.

Then the Mallas, with eyes reddened like bulls, slowly bore the bier, while musical instruments *(turya)*, pleasant to the ear, sounded in the sky like clouds in the rains.

Divine flowers, lotuses and every kind of bloom, fell from the sky as though shed by the trees of the garden of Gitraratha(?), when shaken by the lordly elephants of the quarters.

The great elephants, born of Indra's elephant, cast down lotuses with jewelled interiors and *mandarava* flowers which scattered drops of water and adhered in falling.

Then the Gandharva queens, whose beautiful bodies were born for the time of pleasure, removed the juice of red sandalwood and threw down white clothes which had been perfected without effort.

Holding fluttering pennons aloft and scattering all manner of garlands about, they drew the bier *(sivika)* for the sake of good fortune *(sivaya)* along the sacred *(siva)* road to the accompaniment of music.

The Mallas, full of devotion, bore it along, doing obeisance hundreds of times because of the Sage's spiritual power and bewailing His decease; and so they carried it through the middle of the city.

Proceeding outside through the Naga gate, they crossed the river called Hiranyavati, and at the foot of the caitya known as Mukuta they raised a pyre (corresponding to) His fame.

Then they heaped on the pyre sweat-scented barks and leaves, aloewood, sandalwood and cassia *(elagaja)* and placed the Sage's body thereon, sighing with grief all the while like snakes, and with unsteady eyes.

Then although they applied a lighted lamp three times

to it, the Great Sage's pyre would not take fire at that moment, like the sovereignty of a king of cowardly *(kliba)* nature, whose never-missing bow is in disorder *(vyakula?)*.

Kasyapa was coming along the road, meditating with purified mind, and it was by the power of his wish to see the holy remains of the dead Holy One that the fire did not burn.

Then at that moment the disciple came up quickly in order to see the Guru, and when he had done obeisance to the Best of sages, the fire immediately blazed up of itself.

The fire burnt up the skin, flesh, hair and limbs of the Sage's body, which the sins had not burnt, but, despite the quantity of ghee and fuel and despite the wind, it was unable to consume the bones.

Then in due time they purified the bones of the deceased Saint *(mahatman)* with the finest water, and, placing them in golden pitchers in the city of the Mallas, they chanted hymns of praise:—

"The jars hold the great relics, full of virtue, like the jewelled ore *(dhatu)* of a great mountain, and the relics *(dhatu)* are unharmed by fire, just as the sphere *(dhatu)* of the chief of the gods (Brahma) in heaven (is unharmed by the fire at the end of the aeon).

These bones, informed *(paribhavita?)* with universal benevolence *(maitri)*, and not liable to burning by the fire of passion, are preserved under the influence of devotion to them (or, to Him), and, even though cold, still warm our hearts.

The bones of Him Who overcame desire and was without peer in the world, cannot, by reason of His spiritual power, be borne even by Visnu's Garuda; yet they are borne by us of the human race.

Alas ! The law of the world has inexorable might, and its power has prevailed even against Him Who had power over the Law, and so theses bodily remains, of Him, Whose fame overspread the whole of creation, are placed in these jars.

His brilliancy was as the brilliancy of another sun, and

He illuminated the earth therewith. His body had the hue of gold, yet the fire has left only the bones remaining.

The Seer shattered the vast mountains of the sins, and, when suffering came on Him, He did not lose His steadfastness; He suppressed all suffering, yet His body was consumed by the fire.

The Mallas are wont to cause tears to their enemies in battle, to wipe away the tears of those who take refuge with them, and to refrain from shedding tears even over a loved one, yet now they mourn, shedding tears on the road."

Thus they lamented, despite their pride and strength of arm, and entered the city as though it were a wilderness, and after the relics had been adored by the inhabitants in the streets, they made a pavilion glorious for their worship.

28

RELICS

For some days they worshipped the relics in due form with excellent ceremonies; then there came for them to the town one after another *(kramena)* ambassadors from seven neighbouring kings,

Then at that time, after hearing them in due course, the Mallas, in their pride and by reason of their devotion to the relics, made up their minds not to surrender them, but preferred to fight instead.

Then on learning of their answer, the seven kings, like the seven winds, came up with great violence against the city called after Kusa, with forces like the current of the Ganges in flood.

Then at the sound of the horses of those kings the townsfolk hurriedly entered the town from the jungle with. terror-stricken faces.. .

Then the kings invested the town, tethering their lordly elephants in the foremost groves, and, arrayed in the style that accorded *(anukula)* with their lineage, they acted in hostile fashion *(pratikula)* to the excellent Mallas.

Then that town descended into affliction, like a woman who meets with grief, flinging up the arms of its roofs and closing, the eyes of its gates, with the beautiful long eyelashes of yaks' tails.

With the seven kings, united in intent *(ekakarya)*, shining in their majesty and flashing with their impetuousness, the earth became as fearsome as the sky, when the seven planets shine together at the same time.

Then the nostrils of the womenfolk even were assailed by the odour of elephants in rut, their eyes by the dust raised by the elephants' trunks, and their ears by the clamour of horses, elephants and drums.

Then in all directions there was fighting at the siege, with the gates half invested and surrounded by elephants and troops of horses, and with the preparation of darts and of blazing liquids in the throwing machines.

Then the citizens abandoned embarrassment out of fear and courage and collected on the ramparts, with lances, swords and arrows, glaring like hawks on their enemies.

Some shouted out in their excitement, so others collecting together blew conchshells. Some flung themselves about violently, similarly others brandished sharp swords.

Then the wives of the warriors, seeing the Mallas about to fight for victory and roaring out their names like wrestlers *(malla),* prepared at the same time their minds, medicines, and rewards (for the warriors).

The womenfolk of the warriors there, ail trembling, bound on the armour of their sons who wished, to go in the forefront of battle, and they performed magic rites for their safety *(santividya?),* while their faces were despondent and their tears unrestrained.

Others, with downcast faces like hinds, in going to their husbands clang to the bow he wanted, and as they looked on the hero whose face was towards the battle, (their steps) were checked and they neither went forward nor stood still.

When the kings saw the Mallas thus arrayed and coming forth to fight, like snakes which have been confined in a jar, they made up their minds to fight.

The Brahman, Drona, saw the chariots, elephants, cavalry and footsoldiers all excited and fully intent on fighting, and out of his learning and loving kindness he uttered these words:—

"You are able on the battlefield to overcome with your arrows the life and fury of your foes, but you cannot do so easily to those who dwell apart in forts, how much less then when your adversaries are all of one mind *(ekakarya)*?

Or if you conquer your enemies by investment, is it right *(dharma)* with determined minds to extirpate them and to besiege and injure the innocent townsfolk ?

Just as when black snakes, entering a hole, meet together on the way and bite each other, either there will be no complete *(ekanta)* victory from the siege, or else the besieged will obtain the victory.

For even men of little worth taking fire on hearing the news of the siege in the town, will come to great worth, like a small fire heaped high with combustibles.

Religious men *(dharmatman)*, though besieged in a town, repulsed by their austerities those who came with intent to kill them, and despite their withered arms they conquered. Karandhama in the city of Kusa by the strength of religion.

Those kings, who acquired the whole earth, whether for fame or for obtaining territory (or, the objects of sense), had to leave it and returned to dust, as oxen, after drinking water from the pool, have to return to the pasture ground.

Therefore seeing rightly what religion and profit *(artha)* require, you should strive by peaceful means (*saman*); for those who are conquered by arrows may again blaze (into enmity), but those who are conquered by peaceful means never change in feeling.

All this is not within your competence, and your forces are not able to meet the enemy's forces. You should practise forbearance in accordance with the teaching of that very sakya Sage, Whom it is your intention to honour."

Thus, although they were kings, did that good man instruct them with decision and tell them of the real good, with all the plainspeaking and lovingkindness of a Brahman. Then they made reply:—

"These words of yours are timely and wise and spoken in friendly fashion for our good; learn now what is the intention of the kings, (which proceeds) from delight in the Law and reliance on their strength.

Men as a rule undertake affairs for the sake of passion, or out of anger, or for their power, or for death; but we, inspired by reverence *(sabhimana)*, have taken up our bows simply in order to do honour to the Buddha.

Sisupala and the Cedis, in taking the sacrificial gifts *(daksina)* for the sake of pride, strove with Krsna; why should we not risk even our lives in order to perform our adoration to Him Who abandoned pride ?

The Vrsni-Andhakas, kings who ruled the earth, came to blows for the sake of a maiden; wliy should we not risk even our lives to adore Him Who overcame passion ?

The very wrathful seer, the son of Bhrgu, took up arms to exterminate the Ksatriyas; why should we not risk even our lives to adore Him Who overcame wrath ?

The Daitya, extremely ferocious though he was, went to destruction by embracing *(parigrah)* death in the shape *(abhidhana)* of Sita; why should not we risk even our lives to adore Him Who abandoned all possessions *(parigraha)?*

Similarly Eli and Paka, with enmity increasing between them, wore destroyed...; why should we not risk even our lives to adore Him Who was free from delusion ?

Those and many other contests that arose in the world had their origin in the faults; why should we not fight, when we are bound by devotion to the Supreme Master and it is to our advantage *(sahita)?*

Such then is our purpose: do you go quickly as our envoy and strive with all your might *(sarvatmana)* that this object may be accomplished without fighting.

Your words, spoken in accordance with religion, have checked us, though we are ready to fight and have sharp arrows, just as spells check snakes, which drink down the poison spreading within them."

The Brahman accepted the kings' instructions with the words, "Thus will I do," and entered the city; in due course he saw the Mallas, and after seeing them he addressed these words to them at the proper time:—

"These kings of men, with bows in their hands and with shining armour glorious as the sun, are at the gates of this city of yours, ready to spring like lions licking their chops.

Having regard to the swords set in their scabbards and to their golden-backed bows, they are not afraid of the challenge to battle, but, remembering the Sage's Law, they are afraid of trespassing against the Law.

'You should respect,' they say, 'our intention in that we have come, not for territory or wealth, nor out of pride or enmity, but because of our devotion to the Sage.

The Sage was Guru to you and us alike; hence this trouble. Therefore the company of brethren have assembled and come here with the sole object of adoring the relics of the Guru.

Miserliness about wealth is not so great a sin as miserliness in the practice of the Law. It is a sin to decide to speak in miserly fashion, and sin is indeed the enemy of the Law.

If your decision is against giving, then come out from the fort and wait upon your guests. Those whose strength is in their gates, not in their arrows, are not born of a Ksatriya family.'

This is the message addressed to you by the lords of men, and it manifests good feeling and courage. I have also considered the matter affectionately within myself, listen then to what I am about to say.

Quarrelling with others makes neither for happiness nor for the Law; do not bear ill-will, but follow the way of peace. For the Sage used to preach forbearance, by which the fire of devotion will ever increase.

Men betake themselves to contention for one of the two; wealth or passion, but for the man who has become saintly *(arya)* for the sake of the Law, religious peace and enmity are said to exclude each other mutually.

It ill accords with your principles to do hurt, while worshipping the Compassionate One, Who, Himself attaining peace, with benevolent mind preached mercy to all beings.

Therefore by the gift of the relics share *(samvibhaja?)* with them fame and the body of the Law. Thereby you will be at peace with them, and they too will gain the Law and fame.

We, as followers of the Law, should unite to the Law, by effort even, those who have fallen away from the Law. For those who unite others with the Law cause the Law to endure.

The supreme holy Seer said that the gift of the Law is the most excellent of all gifts; anyone may give wealth, but the giver of the Law is hard to find."

Then, when they heard from the Brahman, who was the peer of Drona in knowledge, the words of the Law, which are renowned and bring pleasure, they looked at each other much abashed and said to him:—

"Ah! Your resolution is that of a good friend and associated with the virtues, as befits a Brahman. We are like bad horses straying down the wrong road, and you have put us on the well-worn track.

We should certainly do as you have said, since it is proper to accept the advice of a compassionate friend. For those who neglect the words of a friendly man afterwards fall into suffering and grieve."

Then the Mallas with devotion and virtue *(guna)* divided the relics of Him Who knew the universe *(lokadhatu)* into eight parts, and then keeping one part for themselves, they handed over the remaining seven to the others, one for each of them.

The lords of the earth too, thus honourably treated by the Mallas, returned joyfully to their own lands, their goal attained. Then with due ceremony they set up stupas in their cities for the relics of the Seer.

Then Drona, wishing to erect a stupa for the Sage in his own country, took the pitcher for his share, and the people named Pisala also, filled with devotion, took the ashes that were left over.

Then at first there were eight stupas, like white hills, which contained the relics. The Brahman's stupa holding the pitcher, was the ninth, and the one which housed the ashes became the tenth.

The kings with their subjects and the Brahmans with their children adored on earth these various stupas of the Sage, which Lad waving flags and resembled the snowy peaks of Mount Kailasa.

The various lords of men paid excellent reverence to the stupas which held the relics of the Saviour (Jina) with the chanting of hyms (?) and the finest perfumes and lovely garlands and the sound of music.

Then in course of time the five hundred Arhats assembled in the town marked by the five mountains, and on the side of the mountain collected the Sage's sermons in order properly to establish the Law again.

The disciples, deciding that it was Ananda who had heard all the sections from the Great Seer, asked the Vaideha sage with the agreement of the assembly *(samgha)* to repeat the doctrine *(pravacana)*.

Then he sat down in the midst of them and repeated the sermons as they had been preached by the Best of speakers, saying "Thus I heard this," and explaining the place, the reference, the time and the person addressed.

Thereby in union with *(anubaddha)* the Arhats he established the scriptures *(sastra)* of the Great Sage's Law, and it is by its full acquisition with effort that men have passed, are passing and will pass beyond sorrow.

In course of time king Asoka was born, who was devoted to the faith; he caused grief to proud enemies and removed the grief of people in suffering, being pleasant to look on as an *asoka* tree, laden with blossoms and fruit.

The noble glory of the Maurya race, he set to work for the good of his subjects to provide the whole earth with stupas, and so he who had been called Candasoka became Asoka Dharmaraja.

The Maurya took the relics of the seer from the seven stupas in which they had been deposited, and distributed them in due course in a single day over eighty thousand majestic stupas, which shone with the brilliancy of autumn clouds.

The eighth of the original stupas, situated in Ramapura, was guarded at that time by faithful Nagas, and the king therefore did not obtain the relics from it; but thereby his faith in them was much increased.

Therefore, although the king retained the sovereignty, which is fugitive, and though he continued to abide among the enjoyments (*phala*): which are the enemies of the mind, yet, without assuming the ochre-coloured robe, he purified his mind and obtained the first fruit.

Thereby whoever anywhere has revered, does revere or will revere the Sage, has obtained, does obtain or will obtain the very highest fruit which is enjoyed by the good.

The wise know the virtues of the Buddha to be such that, given equal purity of mind, the same fruit will be won either by reverencing the Seer during His worldly existence or by doing obeisance to His relics after the Parinirvana.

Therefore one should ever pay reverence to the lofty-minded compassionate Sage, the best Object of worship, the Knower of the excellent Law, which is supreme, immutable, never tailing and profitable.

Why should it not be right in this world for wise religious men, who know what He did, to present a thank-offering to Him Who for others' good underwent the greatest toil in His compassion and in His supreme knowledge of the dispositions of men ?

Seeing that on earth there is no danger like that of old age and death, and in heaven like that of the fall therefrom, what good man is to be so worshipped as He Who ever recognized these two dangers of the universe ?

So long as birth exists, unhappiness is produced, and there is no bliss to compare with that of freedom from new existence; what good man therefore is to be so reverenced as He Who obtained this freedom and it to the world ?

Thus this poem has been composed for the good and happiness of all people in accordance with the Sage's Scriptures, out of reverence for the Bull of sages, and not to display the qualities of learning or skill in poetry.